"As a father, I see the impact of social media and other influences on my kids' lives, and it's not always positive. Makaila Nichols shoots straight in *Blatantly Honest* about the pressures of growing up in such a highly social climate and offers much-needed advice for other teens."

—David Boreanaz, actor, director, producer of film and television

"It's a daring undertaking to be honest about ourselves, especially in the time we live in now. Nothing out there is real anymore; every picture gets retouched. How can a young adult be inspired? In her book, Makaila genuinely shares her experiences. It is such a true gift to her peers for them to realize that we all deal with our insecurities. Teaching us that life is a journey with ups and downs and that we just need to be kind and humble to each other and to ourselves to be able to create a healthier and happier future."

—Frederique van der Wal, super model and entrepreneur

"By sharing her story, Makaila is helping other teens know they aren't out there alone in trying to maneuver through tough situations like bullying. She knows what she stands for and is using her voice to encourage others to do the same. Because real change takes courage!"

—Shawn Edgington, author and founder of
The Great American NO BULL Challenge

"Pressure. Obligations. Being on display. Welcome to today's teenagehood. And who knows it better than teen model and actress Makaila Nichols. *Blatantly Honest* makes you feel like you're talking with an older sister or a close friend—but this isn't your mother's advice. Times have changed. Today's world is different. It's high time that your advice catches up."

—Anna Caltabiano, teen author of The Seventh
Miss Hatfield trilogy and media influencer

"Growing up in the spotlight, I have always been criticized for my body and held to impossible standards. Bullying comes in all shapes and sizes. You can either let it tear you down or you can use it to motivate yourself toward success. I know Mak personally and professionally, and she is a great example of being courageous enough to speak up. I think she will leave a lasting impact on the next generation."

—Sophie Simmons, actress

BLATANTLY HONEST

Safiye,

I hear you are quite the remarkable young lady! Your Mom is so proud of you & all you do! Never let anyone try to stop you from achieving your dreams! You can set your mind to anything and more importantly achieve anything! The world & I are cheering you on. Plus, everyone in your life! Stay true to you &

Never give up!.

Best!

BLATANTLY HONEST

Normal Teen, Abnormal Life

MAKAILA NICHOLS

BROWN BOOKS
PUBLISHING GROUP

Blatantly Honest
Normal Teen, Abnormal Life

Brown Books Publishing Group
16250 Knoll Trail Drive, Suite 205
Dallas, Texas 75248
www.BrownBooks.com
(972) 381-0009

A New Era in Publishing®

ISBN 978-1-61254-918-7
LCCN 2016938289

Printed in the United States
10 9 8 7 6 5 4 3 2 1

For more information or to contact the author, please go to www.MakailaNichols.com.

DEDICATION

To teenagers: These years will fly by so quickly, and, in a blink of an eye, you'll be an adult. When it feels like the world is crumbling down, don't be scared; you're not in this alone.

To their parents: Remember that you were once in their shoes. They need you now more than ever.

CONTENTS

ACKNOWLEDGMENTS

Never in a million years would I have imagined I'd be where I am now. As I look back at all that I have accomplished thus far in my eighteen short years, I see that there are certain people who have influenced my life for the better. I would not be where I am today without help from the following:

My parents, who have guided me to become the best possible version of myself. Even when I've made mistakes, they have shown me how to learn from my errors and move on. They have been my shoulders to cry on and my closest friends, and they loved me when it felt like no one else did.

My grandparents, who have taught me many valuable lessons, including my Papa Fred, whom I lost a few years back. I wish he could see everything I have done.

My teachers from Windermere Prep, who helped me become who I am now even when I couldn't be in the classroom. They allowed me to follow my dreams while still teaching me valuable lessons, and that is something I will forever be grateful for.

The people I have met in the modeling industry have also inspired me to share my story, both the good parts of it and the bad. Their words have made me want to be more than just a pretty face.

Above all, I would like to thank those who did not believe in me. They have given me the motivation to do more, be more, and expect more from myself. And to those who chose to stand by my side, thank you.

1

JOURNEY

"Life is a journey, not a destination."
—Ralph Waldo Emerson

My modeling career started off as a lucky accident. It was mid-October, and I was minding my own business in the Mall at Millenia in Orlando, Florida, with one of my closest friends, Kate. We'd spent the entire day looking for Communion dresses. Tired and frustrated, we'd almost given up. But while we were going from store to store, we had a feeling we were being followed. I noticed a short, bald man who seemed out of place, given that he kept showing up in all the stores I was shopping in.

While Kate was in the dressing room, the man approached me. He came off as quite awkward, which made me feel uncomfortable. The man introduced himself as Keith and said he was an independent model scout for an internationally recognized company. Very nervous and clearly very skeptical, I attempted to leave. Yet he continued to badger me about taking his card. I agreed and promised that I would talk to my parents about his company and that we would get back to him.

At the end of our shopping day, we were exhausted and went home. I had completely forgotten about my meeting with Keith. I went into my room and excitedly unpacked all my bags; then I got dressed to go eat dinner with my parents. As I was taking off my jeans, Keith's business card fell out of my back pocket onto the floor. I stared blankly at it for a moment but then felt compelled to pick it up.

During dinner, my parents noticed I was preoccupied. I told them about my encounter with the man in the store. They were immediately suspicious. Since I am an only child, my dad is clearly overprotective; thus, he launched a thorough investigation into Keith and the company Keith worked for. By the end of Dad's investigation, Keith had allayed my father's suspicions, and my dad was very comfortable with what Keith communicated to him.

This conversation turned into my dad agreeing to invest in my career as a model. In mid-November, I went to the Swan and Dolphin hotel for Keith's modeling workshop.

The first day of the workshop was dedicated to current models. They sat on the stage and talked about how modeling had changed their lives. Once the girls had finished their interviews, a runway coach taught us how to walk the catwalk. I hadn't realized how hard it was to walk in a pair of clunky heels—maybe because I'd never been much of a girly girl and didn't often wear them. I mean, at five feet ten inches, I was already taller than all of my friends and most of the guys in school. Why would I ever wear heels? I hated my height, so I felt awkward trying to walk sexily down an elevated strip of wood. Some of the attendees looked like they'd been practicing their walks forever, and in that moment, I felt totally unprepared.

I noticed that everyone at the showcase—girls and guys—seemed highly competitive. I'm competitive, but I felt that these boys and girls were competitive to the point that it came off as rude. I knew it was just because of their own insecurities. We were all in the same boat; none of us knew what the panel we'd walk in front of the next day wanted. Moreover, I didn't even know who would be on this panel.

The following day, I found myself in front of representatives from the top modeling agencies in the world: Ford, Trump, IMG, Elite, Wilhelmina, NEXT, etc. More than two hundred girls, including myself, were asked to walk out on a runway in a simple tank top, jeans, and a pair of heels. Truthfully, we paid to walk in front of the agencies' top representatives in hope of being discovered. A sense of power and an instant flood of passion came over me the first time I walked on the runway. I felt confident, not like my usual gawky fourteen-year-old self. That's when I knew I wanted to pursue a career in modeling.

After our brief walk, we all waited anxiously while the agents deliberated. The two hundred modeling hopefuls and their parents waited in a massive room. It was dead silent; there were so many faces full of fear and hope. Mid-silence, the runway coach stood on the stage and gave the speech that no one wanted to hear. She talked about how everything happens for a reason while making awkward eye contact with pretty much everyone in the audience. I felt sick. As she made eye contact with me, I knew this had to be the end. I wondered why the agents would pick me anyway. What made me special? I was just a gawky kid, not a model.

Finally, the representatives from each agency were escorted back to their seats. Each contestant was given a number. If your number was called, you were asked to walk to the stage and receive a callback slip from the agency that wanted to see you after the show. I vividly remember my parents telling me that if I didn't get a callback card, it wasn't the end of the world. At first, I kept hearing other numbers being called, but not my number: 314.

Then I heard it. To both my parents' and my surprise, as the calls continued, I got card after card from different agencies. I felt the desperate eyes of the other hopefuls looking at me. I'd befriended a girl next to me with beautiful brown hair, big blue eyes, and infectious smile. Unfortunately, my new friend did not receive a single callback card. I couldn't believe it. Whether or not she was happy for me, I'll never know. Kindness in competition, however, is never forgotten. I often wonder about her. She doesn't even know that she made the most terrifying experience of my life almost bearable. Two of the most important lessons I learned from my new friend are that kindness goes a long away and how important having friends can be.

As the callback process drew to a close, I had ten cards in my hands. Ten of the twelve agencies in attendance wanted to see me. As I sat in my seat, holding the callback cards, I appreciated the surreal moment. After the callback numbers had been read, the runway coach asked those who'd received callbacks to remain in the room; the others were dismissed. I've never seen so many people cry. Parents comforted their children as more than two hundred people left the building. There were twenty other girls and guys left in the room. I still felt out of place. Surrounded by conventionally beautiful faces, I wondered what the agents had seen in me. Was this all a joke—a scam to get my parent's money? I was beginning to think so; yet the agents seemed convinced. In that moment, I realized that maybe they weren't looking for breathtaking beautiful and instead wanted "different." They wanted a young girl who had not hit puberty yet, which is ideal in the fashion industry (as previously mentioned by the runway coach). I was but a blank canvas because my body lacked curves and was the perfect hanger for fashion. I was different, and I fit the mold they so desired.

All of the agents I talked to wanted me to sign with them. Each one offered different promises of travel, luxuries, and opportunities. Keith pushed me toward Wilhelmina Miami. He advised me to take their offer because they were closer to home than most other agencies and extremely well regarded. I took his advice, and they told me to drive down to Miami a week later.

On this first trip to Miami with my parents, they kept reminding me not to get my hopes up. I was so nervous but timidly excited. We drove more than four hours from Orlando for a three o'clock meeting. Wilhelmina's office was buried inside the third floor of the Mondrian Hotel in Miami. The building itself was stunning, looking like it had been crafted by the most contemporary designers in Miami. Yet the hallways were dark and lit by lights that resembled torches. My parents and I got out of the elevator and began what seemed like the longest walk of my life. When we finally reached the end of the hallway, there was a dark door with a giant white logo that read *Wilhelmina Models*. The daunting name was so intimidating that I immediately felt sick to my stomach. Behind that black door was a room full of people who could change my life. I was scared, excited, and anxious all at the same time.

Behind the door was an office, open and welcoming. I walked in with my parents and talked to the director of the agency. She was a matter-of-fact woman who told me she loved my look and asked to take my digitals (natural, no-makeup photos) in a swimsuit.

After the photo shoot, she asked me to follow her into the restroom. I was still wearing my swimsuit at the time. She then pointed to a scale and asked me to step on it. I didn't mind. I considered myself skinny. After all, I was an athlete who played volleyball and did track and field. She told me I weighed 137 pounds, which I already knew. I worked with a trainer at a local Lifestyle fitness center and thought I was in really good shape.

The director of the agency, whom my mom and I nicknamed the "Dragon Lady," told me to lose weight. She said that if I wanted to become a successful high-fashion model, I needed to weigh in at no more than 125 pounds, regardless of my height or muscle mass. Because I was a fourteen-year-old with a dream, I told her I could lose the weight, no problem. She seemed pleased and sent me on my way back to Windermere, the small suburb of Orlando where I live, with a signed contract.

At the time, I thought it'd be easy to lose twelve pounds. I figured if I didn't eat and worked out all the time, I would drop the weight in no time. Man, was I wrong. I found myself eating at least six times a day, doing two brutal workouts a day, wearing sweat suits, drinking distilled water, and spitting into buckets to lose every ounce of water weight possible. A month later, I was 126 pounds. My bones touched the surface of my skin on my back and ribs, and my face was more chiseled than usual. My skin had also turned a yellowish color, signifying that my body was facing malnutrition. My parents seemed disgusted, but I thought I looked like a million bucks.

After I lost the weight, the agency requested I come back to Miami. They wanted to set up what was to be my first test shoot, which is something models do to begin to build their portfolio (also referred to as their "book"). They work with a photographer to capture different looks and styles that are natural yet formative for fashion clients. The Dragon Lady set up three test shoots to begin the process.

When we got to Miami, I strutted into the agency with confidence and jumped onto the scale. My agents were all impressed. They told me I was going to be the next "big star."

The day before my week of test shoots, the agency had set up what seemed like a spa retreat. They highlighted my hair—a first for me—and dyed my eyebrows a less intense shade of brown. I also received a sun-kissed spray tan and had a teeth whitener plastered onto my virgin teeth. It was fun being treated like a superstar.

My first photo shoot was incredible. I'll never forget it. The makeup and hair stylist treated me like I was a piece of art, a modern muse. A flamboyant wardrobe stylist dressed me in expensive clothes I would have never worn in a million years, and the foreign photographer showed me how to use my body to create beautiful angles. When we wrapped the shoot, the photographer waltzed over and rewarded me with Krispy Kreme doughnuts—a whole box of them.

Doughnuts? It seemed like a contradiction. I thought models weren't supposed to eat junk food. Ever. Why would he give me this? It was like giving an entire chocolate cake to someone who's trying to lose weight. It made no sense. But it was hard to resist a box of warm, freshly made glazed doughnuts . . . So I had two.

Abruptly and immediately, I regretted it and excused myself to the bathroom. I had to go to the agency after this shoot, so I plunged my fingers down my throat. I remember getting down on my knees and staring blankly at the toilet bowl. The moment I decided to make myself throw up was a mental battle against my body's natural instinct to keep food in and use it to nourish my body. I held my fingers in my throat until I couldn't get air. Tears welled in my eyes, and I felt the mascara trickle down my powder-stained cheeks. I think that was the exact moment when I began to despise the fashion industry, so quickly after I fell in love with it. Due to my perception of the false ideals that the industry was forcing on me, I found myself choosing to throw up after consuming two doughnuts after a hard day's work with no other food. Pretty messed up, if you ask me.

After my visit to the bathroom, I put on my best smile, ate a breath mint, and said good-bye to the team. When I got in the car, my parents were eager to hear about my first photo shoot. They'd decided not to come with me because they'd been warned against becoming stage parents. I told them that I'd gotten to wear exquisite outfits and beautiful makeup and that I loved being in front of the camera. I truly did love everything about the beauty of fashion, even if I had to work out and diet aggressively in order to feel perfect. I then pulled out my iPhone and shared the behind-the-scenes photos with them. Yet I left out that I'd eaten doughnuts. I didn't want them to know about my recent trip to the bathroom.

My parents then took me straight from the shoot to the agency. As we walked down the dark hallway, I began to feel ill for the first time. I felt something that I was unfamiliar with—lightheadedness. There was nothing I could do about it, though, because I had a meeting with the Dragon Lady.

When I pushed open the dark, intimidating doors, I saw a few other models in the office. They were all tall, thin, and beautiful. But honestly, they looked like they could use something to eat. I threw out what I'd once thought was the ideal version of the perfect woman, who were skinny and sickly, and instead idolized women who were tall and fit and had sun-kissed skin. After all, that body type is what society views as ideal. Is that because this is how the top models look? I felt that if I could look like those girls, I would become a supermodel too. The girls that I saw in the office that day are some of today's most successful models, but it makes me wonder: What did they have to do to themselves to look like that? A boob job? Some plastic surgery? Maybe rib removal? That may sound crazy, but believe it or not, both plastic surgery and rib removal are common in modeling. I had no idea at the time that these practices even existed. I thought that people were built the way they were, and that was that. However, my young mind soon became exposed to things I'd had no idea existed.

The Dragon Lady whisked me away into the conference room a mere fifteen minutes later. There, she took some more digitals of me and gave me what was meant to be a "heart-to-heart." She saw potential in me and seemed entirely impressed with the hard work I had put in to reach my goal. Then she smiled and said, "We will be seeing you soon, Mak." This left me hopeful.

I believe it was fate that Keith found me in Macy's on that hot summer day. But things haven't always been like this for me. I've been very lucky . . . Despite starting a modeling career at fourteen, I've encountered many of the same issues as other teens when it comes to trying to be perfect. I've been made fun of for my looks and verbally abused because of the unique factors that make me who I am. There are some lessons I wish I'd known back then that I'd like to share with you now because you deserve to hear them as much as anyone else.

2
BULLYING

"Makaila is the biggest whore at school."
"Eat some food, you look disgusting."
"Kill yourself, no one likes you anyway."
"I hope you die."

What makes one person superior to another? Nothing. We're all equal, yet we choose to tear each other apart. Over the past eighteen years, I've seen people act out against others on their own personal vendettas. While people give various excuses for bullying, it usually comes down to the bully's troubled home life, past incidents, jealous tensions, or personal insecurities. If you've bullied someone for one of these reasons, or maybe one not listed here, please know I'm not here to condemn you. Rather, I'd like to help you identify why you pick on others with the hope that together we can put a stop to bullying once and for all.

I'm going to be honest with you. I've been bullied. I'm not asking for your sympathy; I'm just letting those of you who've also been picked on know that I understand. I know how it feels. Since I started school, people would make fun of my speech, hair, sharp-ridged teeth, glasses, and braces.

As a little kid, I was nowhere near perfect, but I was happy with who I was. I always had my face in books about dinosaurs, socks on my hands, red lipstick on my nose (because I wanted to be Rudolph the Red-Nosed Reindeer), and I couldn't have cared less what people thought of me. I liked what I liked, and I wore what I wore. Little did I know that the things I liked would be so hated by my peers, many of whom rattled me with their constant insults. At the time, I didn't know there was a word to describe what was happening to me. I was simply a child who had no idea how people could say such mean things, and I would never have guessed that their words would follow me the rest of my life.

People assume that only certain types of kids are bullied. The kids with glasses, the nerds, the overweight—but really, kids will find any excuse to bully you if you're different. Sometimes the thing that makes you different is a source of jealousy to others. I believe this can be a strong motive behind bullying. I've seen it happen to myself and to others, and although I hate to admit it, I've been guilty of it as well.

In middle school, kids began to bully me because my home life was different from theirs. My father is an extraordinarily hard worker and was able to provide our family with experiences most of my classmates didn't have access to. I loved all the things I got to do as a kid, all the concerts and sporting events, but I would find myself crying at home after school almost daily. I still look back on this and ask myself, "Why did I bother crying over things that should have made me happy?" The only answer I can come up with is that other kids were jealous and wanted to make me feel bad. My "friends" wanted to make me feel like an outcast because they couldn't relate to me. They assumed I thought I was too good for them, but that was never the case.

I remember going to my first Hilary Duff concert with my parents. My dad's assistant's husband happened to be her tour bus driver. I was able to hang out backstage, go on the tour bus, and meet Hilary. When I told my friends about the experience, they shunned me. So I found myself sitting alone at the lunch table for a while, yet again. A few weeks later, I confided in my parents and told them what was going on. They understood at once and took the time to explain to me about jealousy. I knew that I would not have had access to those special privileges without my dad's hard work, but the other kids didn't know—or care about—the struggle he went through to get to where he is now.

There was a point in my father's life when he was homeless and had no money, but he was determined to make something of himself. He worked hard in the most honest way possible, and sometime later, he became successful despite countless amounts of rejection. I believe his drive came from his desire to give his future family the world, even though I was still only a distant thought in his mind. By the time my parents got married, he could support my mom. Eventually, I came along. He worked so hard, and I often overlook his dedication to our family. You don't learn how to be a hard worker in school. That's something our parents instill within us at home. Or don't.

So I was bullied as a kid because my dad worked hard to give me an extraordinary life. I'd done nothing to deserve it and always strived to keep my privilege from alienating my peers. However, all through middle school, the other kids continued to single me out for the one thing I couldn't change about myself: my life circumstances.

Jealousy will not change the fact that someone gets to do or have something and you don't; it will only make you bitter about it. I guarantee that person may also want something you have. It's a two-way street. We're all guilty of jealousy, but some people are better at controlling their feelings.

There are different forms of bullying, including physical, verbal, and cyber. Physical bullying occurs when any physical damage is done to someone else. According to the National Education Association, "160,000 children miss school every day due to fear of attack or intimidation by other students."[1] Verbal bullying relates to slander or saying hurtful things. Finally, cyberbullying is just what it sounds like—abuse that happens over the Internet: "39% of social network users have been cyber bullied in some way, compared with 22% of online teens who do not use social networks."[2]

In high school, I just so happened to be that one girl—you know, that one kid you always heard about. The one who everyone had a problem with for some unknown reason. That one kid who stands out in the crowd. I found myself a target of the same group that harassed me in middle school. I am an almost-six-foot-tall creature who has a small frame, blonde hair, and hazel eyes. I can't hurt a fly, earned the nickname "Gentle Giant," and always try to put other people first. Despite my efforts, however, people found reasons to hate me. No human is perfect; we all have flaws; yet we still waste our time picking others apart for theirs.

I remember eating lunch everyday with my small circle of friends. We were those three awkward kids who kept to themselves with their heads down. If we were in a stereotypical teen movie, we would've been "the loners."

Occasionally, the popular girls would come over and harass me about the food I was—or wasn't—eating. There was one occasion when I happened to be eating alone. The infamous group of girls came over with a large bag of potato chips, and I was slightly confused as to why they would (a) approach me and (b) have such a large bag of chips. The next thing I knew, I was covered in salty crisps. The girls whipped out their iPhones and snapped away, laughing. I held back my tears because I didn't want them to know they had gotten to me.

I doubt the people who cared so little for me in high school will care enough now to listen to what I have to say in this book. But I listened. I listened, and I remember every painful word. I wrote it all down. Their words fueled my life's fire, and my journey to heal from those words allowed me to blossom into who I am today. Some of those words I still carry with me every day.

"Makaila is such an egotistical and narcissistic bitch."

"So-and-so got a girlfriend and I am not happy about who it is."

"You're such a fake person and were never my best friend."

"I am glad Makaila doesn't come to school anymore. Life is better with her gone."

"You changed so much and became such an asshole. Who are you?"

"Makaila Nichols is the biggest slut. I bet anyone could get it from her."

"I hope you die alone."

"Who do you think you are?"

These are some of the insults I've recorded from social media. Some of them were said by close friends, others by people I've never spoken to. Yet all of these words formed a false projection of who I am as a person. For the record: I do eat food, I will die someday, and no, I don't sleep around.

When I look back at my years in school and the people who made up my small campus, I realize it could've been much worse. I hear horrific stories about school shootings, suicides, and revenge murders. According to the National Voices for Equality Education and Enlightenment, "100,000 students carry a gun to school each day." Suicide is a common result of bullying: "Suicide rates among ten- to fourteen-year-olds have grown more than fifty percent over the last three decades."[3] Luckily, that hasn't plagued my small town. In a sense, I'm thankful that I was the one who got bullied over someone else. I was forced to grow a thick skin and have become who I am because of those who tried to tear me apart. I am strong—I can say that about myself with confidence. I learned how to take criticism early on, and this proved valuable as I pursued my modeling career. I remember the day I got back to school after my first trip to Miami. My peers had seen Instagram photos I'd posted of my photo shoot and seemed dumbfounded, jealous, and intrigued. Suddenly, lots of people wanted to be my friend—even those who'd bullied me.

Every time I booked a job, my first thought was to show those who'd bullied me that I could still be successful. At first, I wanted to tweet or make a post about my new ad in their favorite store, but I also wanted to get away from all the petty bullying tactics, not become part of them. I knew that my success was beginning to intimidate my bullies, but they still lashed out against me on pretty much every social media site you can think of: Instagram, Facebook, Twitter, Tumblr, etc. Because social media is everywhere, it's tough to ignore hateful messages, tweets, or posts directed toward you. It truly feels like harassment, and it can become a nightmare.

You Are Not Alone

If you can relate to this, just know you're not alone. Cyberbullying occurs every day, and it absolutely hurts. It doesn't matter if the words are said directly or indirectly because they will still get to you. I used to lie in bed and cry. I took the words to heart, and then I started to write them down. I wrote the words that broke me on sheets of paper and read them when I needed motivation to prove them wrong. Truth is, only I know who I am deep down. That's the truth for you too.

I know it's tough. Sometimes, the words will get to you. There was a point in time when I thought to do the worst. I thought that maybe the world would be better with me out of the way. Yet the more I thought about it, the more strength it gave me to push on. Cowards quit. Real courage is gained through withstanding difficulties. We all have families who love us, whether we realize it or not. After all the abuse and cowardly attacks, I found myself becoming a more forgiving person because people deserve second chances. We're all human and all make mistakes. I always tell myself, "If we cannot forgive others, how can God forgive us?" I'm always on the lookout for those who need forgiveness and a friend. The bullies are the ones who are typically the loneliest. The bully may or may not be at his or her own breaking point and in desperate need of both friendship and forgiveness.

I realize that hate will continue to dominate the world so long as imperfect people occupy it, but do your own part to make sure you're not contributing to this. If you're someone who feels the need to lash out at others because you're not happy with your life, please realize you could potentially cause someone to harm or kill him or herself. Could you live with that? Could you live with the fact that you are the reason behind why someone cries at night? Or that you tore a family apart because your target took her own life? What about her family? Think before you speak, or simply keep your mouth closed.

We should protect those who need it most. Who cares if you miss a few hours of sleep to talk someone out of doing something they'd regret? If you can save someone's life, do it. Life is always worth saving. The hate from others continues to this day, and it will never stop, but we can choose how to deal with it.

If you're being bullied, *please* ask for help. It's okay to talk to someone—anyone. If you want to talk to me about what's going on, go to my website (www.MakailaNichols.com) and contact me. I'll do my best to answer. If you need to, use the numbers below. That's why they're there. People love you and want to help.

National Suicide Prevention Lines
800-SUICIDE (784-2433)
800-273-TALK (8255)
National Hopeline Network, Suicide & Crisis Hotline
800-442-HOPE (4673)

Anti-Bullying Websites

www.NoBull.org   www.StopBullying.gov

Forgiveness

There's no excuse for bullying someone. We all look different, talk differently, and think different thoughts. There's nothing about us that's the same, except the fact that we're human. It's natural for us to be jealous of others. There are loads of people I wish I could be for a day, but that will never happen. At the end of the day, all you have is yourself.

When I was young, my dad used to say, "People want you to succeed but never more than they do." At first I had no idea what that meant—what did being successful even mean? Now that I'm older, I understand what he means. It's a shame that we, as a species, cannot be happy for others when they surpass our own successes.

Change your life to be the person you want to be. Follow your dreams, and stop tearing others down—it won't make you more successful. Try to be happy for others' successes. If you believe in yourself and someone is trying to tell you that you can't do it, prove them wrong. You will only be as good as you allow yourself to become. As you become successful, don't allow yourself to hold grudges against those who were mean to you; everyone deserves forgiveness, but that doesn't mean you have to forget what you've been through.

If you are being bullied in high school, middle school, home, work, etc., speak up. Do not allow yourself to fall victim to someone else's insecurities. You are worth so much more, and so are other people. If you see someone else who is being bullied, help that person. Kindness goes a long way and can save lives. At one point in my life, I too was afraid to speak up. However, when I look back on it, these incidents have given me strength to stand up for myself. I know that I will not stand for anything less than excellence. Neither should you.

I wrote the following words for those who have bullied me. If you want, you can take my words and apply them to your own bullies.

I forgive you. If you bullied me as a kid or will bully me in the future, I forgive you for picking on me because of your own insecurities. I am not perfect; I will never claim to be. But I can promise you that I am happy with myself. I love my life, and your words will never take that away from me. I hope you can find the happiness I have with myself. Please stop tearing other people down; there is no point. Life is too short to take away from someone else's life. There was a time when your words affected my personal life. There was a time when it got to me. That time is over now. I have forgiven you. Can you forgive yourself?

#BeenThere

I can tell you so many stories about how bullying affected my middle-school and high-school years. From kids picking on me for what I was wearing to being teased because of my weight and even being physically tormented by my peers, everything that happened to me has shaped who I am today. I was picked on mostly because of my weight—something with which I will always struggle in my life and with which I know so many others struggle as well. I remember going on a field trip in the fifth grade to an aquarium. When we got back, the teacher asked what we saw during our adventure. One boy shouted out, "We saw Laura's family, the whales." I was mortified. I felt my face get red and shrunk down in my seat as the other kids laughed at my expense. Occurrences of this type were quite common, but you never really get used to the pain you feel. Another instance occurred in the cafeteria. One of the kids tampered with the chair I was about to sit on. When I sat down, the chair broke, and I fell to the floor. This time, I had a bigger audience that laughed at my expense. It took me a while to recover from that. I've had gum put in my hair that took hours, a lot of peanut butter, and several showers to get out. I've been called more hurtful names than I can even remember. I've been pushed and tripped. The list could go on and on.

It took me a while to come to terms with what I went through for years. When I got to the other side, I learned a lot about myself and why I was targeted. I had no confidence in myself, and the bullies preyed on that. I gave them the power to hurt me. I obviously could not see this at the time, but I would encourage anyone getting picked on to stand up for him or herself and have confidence. Ignoring the bullying will only force you to internalize the pain, and that's not fair to you. Speak up and speak out. Even if you have to fake it until you make it, exude confidence and surround yourself with people who appreciate how special you are.

—Laura Richardson,

senior relocation specialist, age thirty-one

3

FRIENDS

As teenagers, one of our biggest fears is that we're alone in this world. It's a strange fear to have, considering we're pretty much never alone. Our parents always seem to be lurking over our shoulders, and people always seem to know more about our lives than we do. We're constantly surrounded by peers at school in volumes we'll never experience again after college. If all of this is so, then why do we feel alone all the time?

Maybe we don't have enough people in our lives that can be considered "true friends." Why do I say "true friends" instead of "best friends"? I don't believe in the idea of a best friend anymore. The word "best" implies superiority to all others, and in friendships, one should never be above someone else. Thus, this is where the "true friend" can be defined. Location, time, distance, and any other obstacles you throw at a friendship become weak if there is a real bond between two people. When people say life gets in the way, sometimes it's just because they're not willing to make an effort. You can't leave friendships up to fate. If people want to be in your life—or vice versa—then they'll make the effort, and if they don't, then they're not worth having anyway.

A true friend can be hard to find, especially as a teenager when everyone is trying to figure out who they are. And even though you're surrounded by peers all day, you don't have much control over who you come into contact with. You could be friends with Suzi Q., who lives down the road, or maybe with the kid who smiled at you in class when everyone else looked down at their phones. Even though your options are limited, creating and investing in a true friend shouldn't be a random choice, and it certainly shouldn't be someone you'd deem your last option.

Ever since I was child, I was a bit of an odd ball. In preschool, I would wear white socks on my hands and make my mom put her cherry-colored lipstick on my nose every single day. I guess you could say I was good at pretending to be something I wasn't. Obviously, I'm not a reindeer, but at the time, I believed I was. I suppose it wouldn't be surprising if I had been seen as someone's last option for a friend, but no one cared at that age. You know why? It's because all kids are awkward. The funny thing about preschool is that it's one of the only times in our lives when we are all in it together: the nose picker, the overly clingy kid, the kid in the cowboy costume, or the one in the cape.

We all played together regardless of our quirks. We were all friends, all shared each other's goldfish crackers, and all hugged one another after a long day. When differences didn't matter, I somehow managed to fit in with my red nose and sock-covered hands.

It was in preschool that I made my first true friend. Her name is Sydney, and we're still friends to this day. Sydney lived a few doors down from my family in our hometown of Buffalo, New York. She was a year older than me, but the two of us were inseparable. We took dance class together, played sports, had sleepovers, and practically spent all of our time together. Our parents were good friends too, so I thought we'd all be together forever. When my family decided to move to Florida, I was devastated. I remember getting in the car to leave our home for the last time. Sydney's family was standing in the yard to wish us goodbye. As our car pulled out of the driveway, I called out, "Sydney!" Tears ran down both our faces, and she disappeared from view. At the time, I thought I had lost a wonderful friend.

A few years later, I was already immersed in the swing of things in Florida. I was still an odd ball, and while I accepted that part of me, I was disappointed that I hadn't made another close friend like Sydney. It's funny how we change as we get older. We split off into groups based on interest, gender, race, etc. Why? What changes in us that we can no longer overlook differences that our younger selves didn't even recognize? Perhaps it's the fact that, as we age, we become more self-aware. We form a definition of "normal" and start to sort people into categories based on that definition.

I definitely veered from most people's definition of normal, so I spent a large portion of my childhood at home, alone, watching Disney Channel movies. Disney films, circa the early 2000s, usually centered on some type of high-school nerd who, against all social odds, made a difference—or a nerd who was bullied but was secretly a superhero. At one point in time, Disney Channel did a great job of creating an environment where everyone was friends by the end of the movie, especially in *High School Musical.* It was a great movie; there was singing, dancing, romance, and a memorable antagonist—the mean, popular girl, Sharpay Evans.

After watching *High School Musical,* I could sense a little Sharpay Evans in just about everyone I met. So many people I knew seemed power hungry, chasing routes to popularity driven by material possessions and social connections. It bordered on obsession. Then again, everything seemed larger than life and dramatic during middle school. I eventually found a few people who seemed untouched by the mania spreading through school, and they became my only friends. We did everything together: went on vacations, went to the beach, and spent so much time at each other's houses that we had our own toothbrushes there.

Because I was in and out of school for modeling, my teachers worked out a plan for me to continue my classes even when I was off working. I never enrolled in homeschooling but instead learned the same materials as my peers on my own. So I guess you could say I didn't follow the same social growth pattern as other kids in my class as we entered high school. I think that's why relationships with people my own age were so difficult for me. Everyone else was concerned about homecoming; I was concerned about booking my next job. They'd talked about who was dating whom; I talked to agents about who was representing whom. No matter how hard I tried not to alienate others, I couldn't help but feel alienated myself. Eventually, even my closest friends felt distant.

When I left for New York City the first time, I didn't fear losing my friends. The three of us had been close since sometime in middle school, and we had all traveled for long durations of time, especially over summer, without damaging our friendship. I was gone to New York City for only three months while working as a fashion model. Three months is one of those odd lengths of time that can seem like a short moment to some and an eternity to others. My summer in New York City flew by for me, but I guess it didn't for my friends.

I understand now that I'd been living in a different world. They went to school every day, followed by after-school clubs and homework, while I traveled and "had fun" all day. At the time, however, I didn't see that, so when the three months were up, I sent them a text letting them know I'd be flying home that evening. Upon my arrival, they surprised me at my house with balloons, cookies, and big smiles—though something about their cheer felt off to me.

After an hour of forced conversation, I realized that they weren't the same—*we* weren't the same. Where there had once been an open connection between the three of us, I now felt a wall impossible to climb. They smiled and acted like everything was okay, but when I watched them pull out of my driveway, I knew that would be the last time they'd ever come over to my house. Then, at school the following day, I saw that they had new friends—friends they'd made while I was absent from their lives. Eventually, they stopped texting me and inviting me to hang out with them.

It felt like we were strangers.

This went on for several months before I finally became concerned enough to confront them about it. If you think your friends are mad at you or that something is wrong, it's always better to ask them about it rather than assume the worst. In this particular case, unfortunately, the worst wasn't far off. They told me I was a horrible person and that they couldn't believe what I'd become. That was when I learned about the rumors. I'd been gone for only three months, but in that time, the rumor mill had been busy weaving all kinds of damaging stories about Makaila Nichols. It was said that I was sleeping with guys to whom I'd never actually spoken; others claimed my career was a joke, and others said I'd become the worst version of myself. My peers ripped me apart, and no one stood up for me in my absence, not even my friends. You know how you should confront your friends for the truth rather than assume the worst? My friends didn't do that, and by the time we talked about it, they'd already bought into the lies.

After that, I felt very alone at school. I made casual conversation with acquaintances to pass the time, but I no longer had true friends. I had other friends, sure, but they didn't go to school with me. My other friends were all older, mid to late twenties, with lives of their own. They weren't there to go through the halls with me as I completed school.

So I was very independent during my junior year. However, in that year, I grew monumentally as a person. I've learned more about myself in the past two years than I believe I'll learn the rest of my life. Clearly, that may not actually be the case, but I'd like to think I've learned a lot. I know what makes me happy, I know I can take care of myself, and in the end, I know everything will turn out the way it was meant to be. I even began to understand what a true friend actually is. A real friend would stand up for me against malicious lies and especially wouldn't spread them.

The next hard lesson I learned about friendship was that some people don't want anything for you, only from you. Part of me wishes I'd never figured that out. So many people will do pretty much anything to get their fifteen seconds of fame by association or will use you for their own personal gain. You don't have to be a fashion model for people to see your success and want to use it for themselves. Maybe you make the big play in a football game, are recognized for an achievement, or start dating someone popular. Some people who normally wouldn't give you the time of day might suddenly want to be your friend or make up from a fight. After my trip to New York, I began to get more modeling jobs, and with that, more success. Soon I found that the same people who'd said such hurtful things about me now wanted to be my friends again.

When I worked in Los Angeles, I had calls from "friends" from home asking about my life or whether I could get them into certain events. These were the same people who'd talked garbage about me a few months earlier. Even one of my old best friends called to tell me she was sorry and that she missed me. She said she'd been acting out of jealousy, but why couldn't she have just said that before? Jealousy is something everyone experiences, but it's not an excuse for turning on a friend and spreading the kinds of lies that she did. She made me out to be someone I never was nor ever will be. Deep down, I feel that she let the rumors she heard at school from others get into her head and change her true knowledge of who I was.

The Bible says God will forgive us, so I try to be someone who readily forgives others. But just because we forgive someone doesn't mean we accept their past wrongs. Our lives are so special, and our peace of mind and happiness need to be protected at all costs. I accepted my old friends' apologies but would not let them back into my life. Frankly, they lost that privilege. Remember: every one of your friends is privileged to be in your life, and it's important to remind yourself of that when people hurt you. I'm not talking about accidental hurt—that's part of being human—but if someone is malicious, there's no reason to stay in that abusive relationship.

Yet sometimes people do genuinely change. Friendships, like all relationships, take effort. Still, sometimes they just don't work out, or you realize that a particular friend is headed in a different direction than you are. There's nothing wrong with that; it's part of life. Just as some romantic connections are doomed to fail, some friendships can't be forced. I have nothing but positive feelings toward the people who've entered and left my life. Sure, some may have said hurtful things to and about me, but that does not make me judge the quality of the person I know they once were. I once chose them as friends for a reason. I will forever cherish my memories with them. People will often fail you, no matter who they are or what role they play in your life. I've failed others, and no matter how hard you try, you'll probably fail someone in the future. We're human, after all. Forgive them so you don't carry the burden of anger, but you don't have to forget the betrayal.

If a friendship comes to an abrupt end due to a feud or a mutual fallout, learn to cherish the memories you once shared with your friend. I can recall memories that to this day put a smile on my face, even though I don't talk to that person anymore. There's nothing wrong with that; it doesn't mean you're stuck in the past or wishing for something in vain. Remember the fun you once had with that person, and remember what made you smile, but also remember that it's okay to move on from being someone's friend. On the side of a church in the

Upper West Side of New York City, I saw a Mother Teresa quote that said: "Some people come in our life as blessings. Others come in our life as lessons." Those words resonated with me. I hope they do with you, too.

It can be easy to wish someone ill, but life is too short to wish others harm. Keep in mind that the people you wish these ill feelings toward once meant something to you. If you wish them pain, then you are just as bad as they are. The Holy Bible states in Luke 6:27: "*Love* your enemies, do good to those who hate you." We're just humans; we're not God. It's not our duty to wish ill feelings upon someone, especially those that we once cared for.

Sadly, true friendship is something so rare and hard to define, I feel like I've only experienced it once in my life. When I left Buffalo, I left Sydney—physically, but not mentally. The power of true friendship never dies, because Sydney and I are still the best of friends. When we speak, it is like I never really left at all. The human connection we can all relate to surfaces from the moment we come into our family's arms. We attach to our parents, to our family, and those whom we grew up around. Are they not friends too?

I clicked with a few people at my school, just as I'm sure you have. On occasion, I would meet other kids in my neighborhood and play with them too. Childhood is a beautiful thing when it comes to making friends. I think it's the only time we can truly be who we are without the fear of being rejected. There's a certain innocence to friendship; it breathes out faith, love, and happiness. As we get older, these innocent friendships are harder to come by.

The people you allow into your life will, in some way or another, affect you as a person. I've tried countless times to ensure that the people I surround myself with are the best for me, and in turn, I try to bring out the best in others. *Tried* is the key word. Not everyone who comes into your life will be a saint or make you a better person. And not everyone will benefit from your influence. But life has a funny way of getting rid of the weeds in your soul's garden while allowing the flowers to blossom.

Your only responsibility when it comes to friendships is to try. Try to understand the other person; try to make them the best version of themselves and point them in the direction of wholesome growth. Remain true to who you are, and hopefully, in the process, you can become a better version of yourself as well. So long as you know who you are and what you want, life will surround you with those people who are meant to be in your life.

True friends will be there throughout the length of your life. The time one is able to put into a friendship shouldn't be the defining factor of keeping that friendship alive. It's too high of an expectation to believe that people should always be there for you. Life's busy and messy. It's not the amount of time you invest in the friendship that really matters, but the quality. Life can get hectic, and time is never on our side, so do yourself a favor and throw that variable out. Your true friends are those you can spend months apart from yet, when you finally get together, feel like no time has passed. They'll always come back in the end.

At the end of the day, if you wear socks on your hands and red lipstick on your nose, or if you like dinosaurs a little too much, look around. Your true friend will be right there next to you, covered in red lipstick too.

4
SEX AND DATING

As of now, I've had five boyfriends. Of those relationships, three were or are serious, including the relationship I'm in now. But the key word to pay attention to here is *had*. I suppose this isn't uncommon. Most high-school relationships end, after all. I'm dating someone else now; he has been one of my closest friends since childhood. In many ways, it doesn't feel like we're dating. We make each other laugh, we fight like siblings, we know everything there is to know about each other (good and bad), and we are next-door neighbors. Sometimes it feels like a movie—like it's too good to be true. We've all heard the saying that we marry our best friends, and some days, I wouldn't doubt it.

Excluding my current relationship, I've often found dating awkward and uncomfortable, especially if it's not with the right person.

Don't get me wrong; dating is great. You get to understand someone else and have someone understand you. People are almost like puzzles; it takes time to figure them out. Sometimes people will fit you, and other times they won't. But that is the magic of dating. Hopefully, you can find someone to open up to and be yourself with. If that person is worthwhile, they will accept you for who you are. You should never have to change who you are just to date someone.

I realize the people I date now will add to my experience of life in general. Sure, the guys I've dated so far will more than likely not include the man I will marry, but you never know. I could be wrong. I know some relationships do last. We don't know what the future holds. My mother always says, "What is meant to be will be."

I've had three boys break up with me. The first time, I had no idea why. Before it happened, I believed I was going to marry that kid because I was a child and thought I was a princess and he was my prince. I thought we only got to date one person. Forever. The second time a boy broke up with me, the guy needed to "find himself." In both cases, I was lied to, because in each instance, I was left for another girl. The third time, the guy turned out to be gay. That threw me for a loop, let me tell you. Quite honestly, it's not wrong to break up with someone if you feel the need to. Regardless of how these relationships ended, I had a wonderful time dating those three guys during high school. They allowed me to realize all the qualities I do not want in a man.

First and foremost, I want to believe that the man of my dreams is out there. I always joke with friends that my Prince Charming is dead in a ditch. Maybe I'll date ten more guys before I find the man I'm supposed to be with. Whatever is meant to be will be. But ladies and gents—make a list, a vision board, something about what you want your partner to have. Don't settle for less. Your vision board may steer you in the right direction when it comes to dating.

Some of my favorite romance authors give me faith in relationships. I want to be swept off my feet, read love letters, or end up with my best friend. Love is not just about sex. Love is more complicated than butterflies in the stomach, stolen kisses by a locker, and notes passed in the hallway. Dating is about understanding someone else to see if you are compatible and whether this thing called "love" you're both searching for could be found in this relationship.

Bouncing Back from the Breakup

Not every man or woman you meet will be worth dating for a long period of time. If it doesn't work out, take this newly found time for yourself and treat it like a mini vacation. Start a journal, sink into a project, or spend a little more time with friends and family. Get your mind off of it, brush it off, and move on.

The first few days after a breakup are the worst, and you may find yourself wondering if the other person is going to call. Most of the time, they won't. It'll continue to feel nearly impossible for maybe the first few weeks. Try to see it as a learning experience because the pain is only temporary.

To this day, I still think about the boys who broke my heart. When you become emotionally attached people, it can be hard to stop thinking about them—especially if they hurt you. Sometimes you can overlook the actions that hurt you, but, other times, you can't. I often wonder what I did that made them break it off with me. It's sad, because when people leave, they often take parts of you with them. You may want to forget them but can't.

Once you've had your heart broken, it may become even harder to let yourself fall in love again. No one wants to get hurt, and now you not only expect it but also know the sting of heartache. But it's good to remember that, as a rule, fear is one of the main reasons we shut people out. We are so scared of taking risks and getting hurt. Some people think teenagers don't understand what love is, but age doesn't limit your ability to feel and give love. To love, age is just a number. We love with all that we can and all that we know.

I believe that, one day, you will find the person you're supposed to be with and grow old together. This person will be the one you take slow walks with around the neighborhood while holding hands. The person who will be the mother or father of your children. Just give it time. Remember: love will always find you, so don't give up on it. If it's meant to happen, it will. Just be patient. Worst comes to worst, you just wait a little bit longer than most.

The greatest advice I can give you about meeting someone great is to date. Meet people. Share memories with someone, and don't spend your life alone. Go out, meet people, and don't shut people out for superficial reasons. You never know who you'll meet. Maybe you will meet the love of your life, and maybe he won't look or act exactly as you imagined he would. The world we live in is a strange place, but then again, love is strange too. Life is too short not to be happy with someone. If you are scared of having your heart broken, just know that it may be unavoidable. It's part of the experience. If you've never had your heart broken, then maybe you were never really in love to begin with.

The only way to give love a fair chance is to give people a chance, and there's no better way than to say yes to one date—a date that may change the rest of your life.

Parents and Dating

Parents are often scared of their children falling in love at a young age because they know how serious it can become. They fear us getting heartbroken or withdrawing from them, but I ask myself whether they remember what they were like as teenagers. Maybe that's *why* they're so fearful. I'm quite certain there are plenty of stories my parents have that they'll never tell me—and that I'll never want to know.

Our parents want us to be open with them. Even when they're being overbearing and critical of our choices, they're just trying to help. And whether we like to admit it or not, there will be times when we need our parents, even when we don't want them around. No one else will be as strong or consistent as our parents when it comes to being the guardian, protector, or shoulder-to-cry-on that we need. Asking for support from your parents can often be hard, especially when they try to warn you about a relationship they know won't end well but that you see as being "true love." Parents hate to see us get hurt, but sometimes we need to get hurt. We need to become strong so we can one day protect our own children.

The Sex Chariot

I believe the media is partially at fault for the concern our parents have over teen dating. If you watch the news, listen to pop music, or watch any movie starring high-school students, you'd see a reoccurring theme that young love is just about sex.

Sex, sex, and more sex.

The media depicts young relationships as being predominately physical. Yes, physical intimacy is part of love; but it's not the only part of a relationship. Our generation's view on the act of sex itself is nothing to brag about. According to the *Huffington Post*, both girls and boys tend to lose their virginity at age seventeen. Sex seems to be more accepted in society than it was when the sexual revolution of the '60s came around. Thus, teens and even preteens of today engage in sexual activity early on. Over the past few years, I've heard many stories from friends and coworkers about their bedroom lives, and from these tales, I've seen one reoccurring theme: sex has lost the one thing it was supposed to express—love. Sex is a conquest that only has one goal, and that's to add another notch on the belt. I've even seen people challenge themselves to bang the hottest person they could find and then never call again once the task is done. Monogamy? Forget it. We as a society are so open to giving ourselves up that it's chipping away at our ability to be truly intimate. We're cheapening sex. What's left to give the person you end up falling in love with? If we continue to devalue ourselves to this extent, aren't we in essence taking something away from our future relationships?

I'm not judging anyone. I believe people should be in any kind of relationship they want. We live in a country where we are free to make such decisions. We have the freedom to choose, and if both parties are happy, then I don't see the problem. I, however, am personally not one to just hook up. I love the thought of having someone by my side when I need comfort and someone to adventure with. Call me old-fashioned, but I like commitment.

I believe that I can speak on behalf of teenage girls everywhere when I say the following: we all want to experience the type of love that inspires romance novelists. As young women, we want to be swept off our feet and cared for. We want someone who makes us feel loved and, more importantly, wanted. In a world where we tend to feel alone, love is what holds everything together.

The media is driving this so-called "sex chariot." We live in a day and age where women use their bodies to sell burgers and beer to men or bras to women who just want to feel beautiful. It creates a culture in which we're meant to show off our bodies in the hope of manipulating someone or getting affection in return. The larger the boobs, the more guys will like you; the larger the butt, same thing. For guys, it's no different. If you have washboard abs or the perfect bone structure, girls will want to be with you.

The industry I am in has made these false standards almost expected. The truth is that we set our standards too high when it comes to wanting to be with a "perfect ten." I have run into a handful of men who wanted to date me just because my job title happened to be "model." In a sense, it's almost sickening. People feel the need to carry their eye candy with them for attention, but, in reality, even those deemed eye candy get confidence issues too.

We've begun to think that if we make it seem like we are putting ourselves out there sexually, then surely we will fall in love. That, however, is not the case. Presenting yourself that way almost guarantees that you will attract someone who is only interested in your body. Yet people are such good liars that it can be hard to decipher everyone's ulterior motives—especially when it comes to the three strongest words in the human language: *I love you*. When we hear those words, we want to believe them. All of us want to be loved, and most of us are willing to do just about anything to have someone say that to us.

However, there is a big difference between saying something you truly mean and saying something to get laid. I've been told by six different guys that they loved me, and most of those guys were only trying to get in my pants. I didn't realize that at the time, of course. Boy after boy, all saying what I wanted to hear. I wanted to be wanted; I wanted to be loved. I wanted the sappy good-morning texts and the cute pet names. People usually pick up on what someone wants versus what someone needs. They will make you believe they want you so that you feel like you *need* them; then you'll do anything to please them just to keep them around.

I learned a lot about the teen sex culture after overhearing a very confusing conversation in middle school. There were some high schoolers talking about their recent baseball plays, but I knew that none of the girls were on the school's team.

The following day at school, I tentatively approached my small group of friends for our morning gossip session. After some chitchat, I shared what I'd overheard the older girls talking about. To my surprise, my friends already knew everything there was to know about the bases, so baby Makaila was given a lesson on the terminology of hookup culture—from the bases to defining "open relationship," "hooking up," and "friends with benefits." I was quite dismayed to hear that people I knew were doing such things, and not only doing them but thinking nothing of it. Maybe I was just a prude. I would kiss lots of boys, but nothing more. I never played baseball in high school.

As an eighteen-year-old, I certainly am not an expert on sex, but I can offer advice based on my experience and the experiences my friends have had. The modeling industry is rife with promiscuity, so you can imagine the stories I've heard. For starters, don't believe anyone when they say how many partners they've had. Remember, we live in the world of the sexual conquest. People will say and do almost anything to get into your pants at some point in your life. You're your own best advocate.

Sure, we all mess up, and we'll all do stupid stuff more than once, but there are always consequences to our actions. Just remember that the consequences of a sexual mistake can last a lifetime and influence not only your own life but others'.

I understand that, in this day and age, we're encouraged to have sex. Sex is all around us. All the movies seem to make fun of the virgins, and those who do embrace their inner sex symbol are revered. Sex is glorified. Therefore, many of us do it with someone who means nothing to us just to fit in—to feel special. No one wants to end up like *The 40-Year-Old Virgin*. Instead, people go to parties on the weekends and get plastered. Then, miraculously, their legs are open and their panties are on the ground. *Boom*. Virginity is out the window. The day after, she may not even remember who she lost it to and . . . wait, was a condom involved?

Goodness. How scary would it be to have to run to your phone and ask your friends what happened? They'd probably all think it was funny.

After an incident like that, you'd immediately have to deal with the fact that you could be pregnant or have a sexually transmitted disease (STD).

Once a year, my school would have a gynecologist present a sex-ed class for all students in the high school. The gynecologist would pace back and forth in the front of the room, preaching the same information that none of us wanted to hear—that, each year, 9.5 million young adults contract a sexually transmitted disease and that abstinence is the only way to truly prevent it.

Condoms and birth control can save lives, literally. Never sleep with someone without a condom—even if you're on birth control—because, remember: birth control does not prevent STDs. Additionally, condoms do not prevent all STDs or sexually transmitted infections (STIs). If you do become monogamous with someone, choose to go on birth control, and plan to forego condoms, make certain that you both get fully screened for STDs and STIs. Human papillomavirus (HPV) can be transmitted even when a condom is used, and HPV can lead to cervical cancer. Men are carriers of HPV, but there is no test to see whether or not a man is a carrier. So make sure anyone you choose to sleep with is worth the risk.

There was a girl who went to my school who became pregnant. I didn't even know she was sexually active, and I never would have thought she would become pregnant. One day, she sat me down and confessed that she'd had an abortion at a local Planned Parenthood and that her parents didn't know. She was scared and hurt all at the same time. She had to play God and decide whether her unborn child would live or die.

My heart broke when she told me that she went through with the procedure. People are not supposed to play God. Her child would never live and never get to walk this earth. The guy she was with never spoke to her again; he walked away when she told him. People always claim they'll be ready to deal with consequences that they think they'll never have to face. Unfortunately, that can lead to playing with a human life.

Sex is meant to be an expression of love. It's not meant to be a hobby or just a way to add notches to the belt. There are real consequences when it's not taken seriously. People can die from sexually transmitted diseases, and unborn children will never get to see the light of day because they weren't given the chance to have a say in their own life. Using protection can stop unwanted pregnancies and the spread of most sexually transmitted diseases. However, nothing is foolproof. I know I sound like a sex-ed teacher from school, but the only way to ensure you will not become a parent or contract a sexually transmitted disease is to be abstinent. Seriously. It may not be realistic to ask all teens to abstain from sexual activity, but everyone must have some level of self-control.

I long to live back in a time when women were courted and men would go to hell and back to prove their love for a woman. Chivalry is dead. People today sometimes wind up having sex with someone after one date. They're so caught up in the moment, maybe feeling especially passionate or excited about the attention, that they forget to value themselves. If you're someone who has fallen into this trap, it's okay. But it's important that you take some time and evaluate why and whether you'd really ever do it again. It's rare today to see a couple wait, and I have so much respect for those who do. But if we work together to change our generation's attitude toward sex, maybe we can find our way back to a time when sex was more meaningful.

Every time I see an older couple holding hands as they walk down the street, my heart melts. I love to hear stories from the elderly about how they met their soul mate in high school or when they were just children. I love to see the look in two people's eyes as they say their vows. Love is beautiful. It exists everywhere. But let's face it: people are not focused on love anymore. The hookup culture is taking over, and it's now more important that we have sex and live noncelibate lives than practice self-control and wait for intimacy. "But we're teenagers!" you say. "Our raging hormones demand sexual satisfaction. Who are we to deny this?" I bet if you ask the old couple walking down the street holding hands, they'd say the wait was worth it.

I know abstinence can be hard because it hurts to be called a virgin or a prude. I get called that all the time, but you know, I'll be happy when I give myself to someone I love. I do everything out of love and respect. I don't want to be another statistic. When you respect yourself and can stand behind the choices you make, the right person will come along. Life isn't a race to have as much sex as possible with as many people as you can. The right time will come eventually, and I can promise you that the right person will be worth waiting for.

Love Yourself

What is love? To be completely honest, I don't think anyone knows the answer to that. Scientists have proven that love is a chemical bond. This book is not meant to be a science class (just a mini sex-ed class for a bit), but here's a fun fact about the chemical reactions you experience when in love. According to *Scientific American,* your pupils get larger when you are with someone you are attracted to. Apparently, they dilate because the eyes want to see as much of that person as possible.

I could see how, to some, dating could be solely about the sex. But I think a lot more of us are just hoping that dating will lead to the person we'll marry. Some people want to find their soul mate as soon as possible. I don't know if love leads to soul mates, but I've learned a few things about love in my limited experience. I've learned that the ones we love are the people we confide in, the people who make us better, and the people we cannot live without. Love is found in the people who make us smile for no reason or who make us do crazy things. Love is different for everyone. Scientists may be able to prove that love is a chemical bond, but I don't think that fully explains why we love *whom* we love or why each relationship affects us differently.

I've learned that love can make you do crazy things. I have written love letters for someone to open every single day for a month and used germ-covered pay phones when I got my cell phone taken way. I've had people deliver gifts for me when I was out of town, and I've jumped on planes to visit family and friends in their time of need. I've learned that love takes many different forms. Even with exes, there may be a point when you'd do anything to try to win an ex back. But I've also learned that, after a breakup, the best cure for heartache is finding yourself. If you love yourself and can handle being alone, you will be happy again before you love someone else. The love you have for your friends and family will help you get through the toughest of times.

Our biggest regrets will be the chances we didn't take. Taking a risk can be scary; trust me, I know. I've had my heart shattered and stomped on and somehow managed to pull myself back together. With that said, go meet people, fall in love, get hurt, and get stronger. You won't know what this world has to offer if you never have the courage to look.

#BeenThere

When I was sixteen, I fell in love. Serious, gut-wrenching, "this is the guy I'm gonna marry" love. I was so in love with this person that my entire life revolved around him. We had all the same friends, went everywhere together, and rarely spent any free time apart. Our families were close, so we even got to go on vacations together. At the very end of my senior year, as we prepared to go off to college and leave one another, without warning and without even telling me what was going on or why, he slept with another girl and decided that she would be his new girlfriend. No explanation, no tearful good-bye; he just fell into her arms and left me, taking all of our friends with him. This destroyed me. I cried for weeks, didn't sleep, and felt a sense of loss I hope to never feel again. But as I got my life back together and my confidence back—losing a little weight and getting some new clothes helped—he came crawling back with a list of excuses and apologies. Of course, I took him back.

The relationship came to a natural end not long after because I could never really forgive him. As I look back, however, I wish I had never taken him back. If I could, I would tell my teen self to stay strong, to be confident enough to be single, and to view him crawling back as the victory. I didn't have to say "yes" to make it count. If I could, I'd also tell myself not to get a tattoo with this person. Probably not the best idea I've ever had . . .

—Alee Anderson,

editor, thirty-one

5

SEXUAL ASSAULT

At one point in my life, I questioned whether or not there was still good in a mankind. We see horrific events happen to people on the television screen, read about them in books, or hear about them through the grapevine, but we never think that terrible things will happen to us. I know I never did.

Life would be so much easier if we were able to explain why bad things happen to good people. I wish I could make sense of the evil in the world and why it will never cease to exist. I wish I could tell you that danger will never find you. Unfortunately, I can't say any of that, because that's not how life works.

There's evil in this world. Real evil encompasses modern-day monsters lurking in the shadows. When I was just a kid, I thought I'd been exposed to this type of evil. I was afraid to go to sleep at night because I feared the dark. I was convinced that a monster would come snatch me and take me. These thoughts occurred when I was four after the September 11 attacks. Deep down inside, I felt that it'd happen again but this time in my own backyard, and I was horrified. My parents tried to comfort me and tell me that the monsters weren't real—but they are.

I've seen things that have opened my eyes to how cruel the world can be. When I was five, I was on the playground with my best friend, Jake. We were pushing each other on the swings, having a normal day at a local YMCA summer camp. Suddenly, out of the corner of my eye, I saw a man in a blue baseball cap leaning up against the closest fence. The man had a handful of M&M's and a seemingly innocent smile. He called us over, and Jake and I both made our way toward him. He made brief conversation, handed us a few candies, and told us that he had more candy in his car. So we went.

Jake led the way, and I followed him into the backseat of a medium-sized Lexus. The car still had that new smell to it and a perfect white-leather interior. The man said he had to close the door so the AC wouldn't escape, so he did. Immediately, the child locks went on. The next thing I remember was hearing a frantic camp counselor shout and run toward the car.

To my immediate relief, it turned out that the man worked at the camp but was incognito. I wasn't actually being kidnapped. The funny thing is that I didn't care about the thought of being kidnapped; instead, I was more afraid of what my parents would say. The main focus of the camp was to instill life lessons in young children. Clearly, Jake and I failed epically.

Silenced

Ever since I was a child, I've seen the potential evils in the world, and my parents have done everything they could to make sure I'd know what to do in a scary situation. However, my little incident at YMCA camp made it appear to me that life was all just a prolonged drill in which nothing bad could actually happen. My parents seemed to dance around the topic of me growing up and being out on my own as if it was always so distant.

I believe that parents' main job is to protect their children; thus, they would do everything in their power to keep us safe (even secret safety camps). Just like in everyone's childhood, everything we did was innocent. Stolen kisses and innocent hand-holding were never overlooked. Every action we took, we did without sin. We knew nothing about what the future encompassed, and we lived in the moment. Childhood is the only time in our entire lives defined by innocence.

The innocence of children is one of the most beautiful human qualities that I have ever seen, but it does not last long. For a few short years of life, we don't worry about the future, death, hatred, or sex in general. In a child's mind, there is no hassle about who looks the best or what outfit makes you appear more promiscuous. Then puberty hits, and all bets are off.

When thinking about safety, the only thing children seem to understand is avoiding taking candy from strangers, watching for cars, and generally staying away from things that could burn or hurt them. They never really consider someone walking into their lives and destroying their innocence, because they live in the moment. For children especially, the present is about happily avoiding danger that they never truly believe will strike.

But when danger does strike, it's hard to overcome. Darkness then seems to encroach upon your entire existence. Do you know what it's like to lie awake at night and wish you could just fall asleep and never wake up? Do you know what it's like to feel so empty inside that nothing even matters? I do. I know it all too well. And it all started because of him—because he told me not to tell. And at first, I didn't dare open my mouth. I was scared. I was scared of what he might do to me if someone found out.

When I close my eyes at night, I'm haunted by those memories— memories of when I lost my innocence too soon. My memories are nothing but horrific. It is ironic that sometimes the people closest to us are the most dangerous. Even those we once considered "friends." I had one such "friend" whose name I will leave unwritten. But he turned out to be the devil in disguise.

Before I started modeling, I was just "one of the guys." I was thirteen and hung out with mainly guys because I enjoyed playing sports. I was never into Barbie dolls or makeup; instead, I liked roughhousing and being outdoors. Naturally, I befriended the new boy in school. He was popular, and all the girls had crushes on him, except me. Before long, he and I were spending a lot of time together, but only as friends. He seemed to have a different girlfriend every week, and the girl was never me. I was only the "friend"—nothing more.

As we got older, I began to notice the way he looked at me, the way he dropped subtle hints about how pretty I looked. I found it odd. A short time after that, he began making slight passes at me, such as a quick peck on the cheek or a slap on the bum. Again, I thought nothing of it. I was just the "friend." I even asked him to stop because I thought it would ruin our friendship. He never did stop; he only joked around and said that he was playing. Just playing . . .

Then something changed. He decided that he didn't want to be just friends anymore. From that moment on, he took advantage of me in more ways than one. I remember being disgusted at the male body as well as my own genitalia. My areas that had once been deemed private were open ground for him to touch and abuse at his convenience.

I repeatedly begged him not to and told him I wasn't ready for these forced advancements. But he told me that if I didn't go along with it, he would hurt me more. He always said that he was "just warming up" and that the real "fun" hadn't begun yet. He said that if I told anyone about his forced gestures, I'd regret it. Funny, because he told people regardless. He told his little football buddies that I was an easy whore. There were days when I thought maybe he was right because I didn't stop him. I let him get into my head, and I let him control me. I never spoke up because I was afraid of what he would do to me and of how much worse it might get.

The crazy thing about fear is that it can make you do almost anything. That said, I put up with this abuse for longer than anyone ever should because I thought maybe he was going through a phase. For some odd reason, I still thought he would return to being my friend. This very thought has devastated me. No amount of counseling is going to make my mind okay. I will never be "all right."

The worst of it all was when my parents found out. The school called them in because they were worried about me. I lied to everyone I knew for almost a year about what had been going on. I didn't want them to be mad at me for not telling; nor did I want them to think I was okay with what had happened to me. There was no easy out for me. I remember when I saw my mother cry that I had to tell the whole truth. To my surprise, my own parents did not believe my story of fear and abuse at first because the rumor mill had said I was a slut. Everyone was in denial, and I was too. I realized how difficult it would be to admit to them, myself, and others that

I had been sexually abused at such a young age by someone I had considered a friend.

As I sat through the meeting with my school's administrators and my parents, I watched my mother's heart break. I felt the urgency of my father's face. The school faculty looked baffled that Makaila Nichols was a victim of sexual assault. They did not know what to think at first; the evidence was buried behind a wall of lies. But when the wall came down, so did my innocence. Innocence dies a harsh death.

I was thirteen years old when my view of love became something less than beautiful. After learning about my prolonged abuse, my parents tried to comfort me. Yet they didn't quite know how. They sent me to a therapist for about a year. However, that abruptly stopped when I thought I was fine. They all tried to make me feel better—they really did. But the verbal abuse from my peers never stopped. I went back to school, and everyone thought I was just the slut I had always been (but never actually was). Some of my peers assumed I'd made the story up for attention. None of the guys had ever been interested in me before, but they suddenly were now. Some even came up with stories about how I'd gotten with them too. But I never had, and, at the time, I was too exhausted to fight off the lies that tarnished my once-prudish reputation.

I began to hate myself. I hated my entire existence. There were weeks in which I would only eat when necessary. There came a point that year at which I didn't want to be alive any longer. I felt defeated.

I felt like garbage, the scum of the earth. Even when I went to bed, I could not escape those empty eyes of his. I was forever haunted. My parents began to notice my rapid decline in health. They took me to a psychologist. I have nothing against psychologists, but as much as they tell you that they understand . . . They don't. So I'd sit there and stare at my doctor in silence. Silence was the only thing that kept me sane because it was the only thing I seemed to know.

The Sun on the Horizon

To this day, I'm not okay. When my boyfriend kisses me, I still clench up. I still have fear that lives inside me. It'll never fully go away. Maybe some of you know this feeling and some of you don't. I hope you will never understand what it is to be scared to love.

I was young when that horrific event happened to me. There was a time when I wished it never did. I know my parents wish they could have saved me from that experience. But at the end of the day, I am a firm believer that everything happens for a reason. What happened to me altered me as a person. I know what the meaning of love is. I know what love should be and what it shouldn't be. Sex itself is meant to be an act of love—not power, possession, or numbers.

Age can't protect you from the evils in the world or the current trends, sex being one of them. Age is but a number. Life won't wait for you to reach a certain age before it drastically changes. My parents had no idea that I had to deal with what happened to me; I never thought it would happen to me. I've learned to expect the unexpected. Life will throw screwballs at you all the time. But what you choose to do with the horrible things that happen to you . . . Well, that says more about you than any event ever could.

I forgive my attacker. I refuse to carry the burden of anger and hatred because of choices he made. I want to be able to move on with my life with the thought that evil will not defeat me.

If something like this happened to you, would you be able to forgive? I know it's incredibly hard to say yes. But forgiveness has helped me mend my thoughts about love. Forgiveness has allowed me to heal in ways I'd never imagined. In my heart, I want to believe that people are good by nature. That's not always the case, but who are we to pick and choose those who are "good by nature"? People make mistakes and often act on impulse. Deep down, I choose to believe that there is good in everyone. I choose to forgive. I shared my story to make sure my loved ones knew so that I could educate them and get the necessary help.

Sexual assault, rape, and abuse occur every single day, and for some reason, there are many people who choose not to report it—perhaps because, more often than not, no one believes them. I once asked, "Why would someone not speak up?" Fear. Fear of the unknown. I know this firsthand. Threats can mentally corrupt you just as harshly as abuse itself. Threats mess with your mental state; they encourage fear. Fear fuels desperation.

I chose not to speak up because I was scared. The threats got to me. Or maybe what kept me quiet was the foreboding feeling that I didn't know what would happen if I spoke up. To this day, I still don't fully understand why I remained silent.

When I look back on it all, I see the sun on the horizon. I am who I am because of my past. I would like to think that maybe I dealt with my pain on the inside so that no one else would have to. I didn't want my family to be in pain, and I didn't want people to feel sorry for me. I did not want people to hate the guy who attacked me. As strange as that sounds, it is the truth. I do not believe in hatred. I believe in resurrection. I hope that he, wherever he is, will learn from his mistakes and become a better human being.

I know there are actual monsters in this world who take advantage of people and get away with it. There has to be an end to it someday. If you're a victim of some sort or know someone who is—please speak up. You could save someone's life. I wish someone had spoken up for me sooner; I wish that I'd had the courage to even do so myself.

I'm eighteen years old. I was thirteen, almost fourteen, when I was assaulted. Take a moment and look at a younger sibling, your own child, or a friend. What if something like that happened to them? There's nothing that would make it okay in your mind. I honestly will never know how my parents dealt with it. Sexual assault does not have only one victim; it has many: families, friends, and even the family of the assailant can all be affected by one unjust action.

Years later, it still crossed my mind from time to time. I realized that one day soon, I could run into him again. We lived in a small town, and he still had friends who went to my school. It was only a matter of time. I used to tell myself that I would be fine and wouldn't think about it if I saw him. But when I saw him last year, things changed.

I was on the school's basketball court, taking photos for the yearbook. Out of the hundreds of blurred faces in the stands, I saw his clearly. It was like a scene from a movie. I froze instantaneously. Why would he be at a basketball game at a school he didn't attend when his school was not playing? It made no sense. A few seconds after I questioned his presence, I felt sick and had to step outside. I found myself bent over a tall bush, throwing up what was left of my dinner.

Three years later, and I still felt sick about it. I know I will see him again. I don't have a clue how I will handle it. I know that time will supposedly heal my wounds, but I don't know if I believe that.

I wish there was a light at the end of the tunnel when it comes to my own personal struggle with sexual assault. I've healed in ways that I never could have imagined, yet I haven't. I still feel the pain. My memories don't fade; only time will tell. I don't dare to bring up the subject to my parents again because it's in the past. Despite the pain and suffering I endured, I feel that my attack happened for a reason.

The thing is, that reason is beyond my reach and even further beyond my control. I'd like to think that telling my story and helping others will help me heal further. I want to be a person someone else can relate to; we all need someone who understands. I may have gone through the same thing as some of you reading this. Despite the differences everyone faces in terms of abuse or tragedy, we all share a common trait: strength. It's not necessarily the shape of the abuse that bonds us; it's the shared experience of enduring something horrific and how we respond. I want all of you to know that it is going to be okay. That's something I still need to tell myself every day. If you can, try to accept the fact that everything happens for a reason. Try to find that reason; try to turn your tragedy into something beautiful or meaningful for you. Every action we take has a consequence or a reward. You owe it to yourself to seek understanding. Despite the horrible events that took place in my life, I've found their true purpose: I am not meant to be silent anymore.

Do not allow yourself to fall silent. Do not put up with anything that will put your body or mind in harm's way. Your body is a temple, and you only have one. No man or woman should ever make you feel any less about yourself or manipulate your physical being in any way. Your body is yours and yours alone, so protect it. However, I know protecting it can be harder than it seems. If someone does take your "innocence" from you by force, do not let them get away with it. Don't blame yourself. It's not your fault. Take control of the present situation, and tell someone.

I'm glad I told my parents. I may have been devastated to confess to them at the time, given that I had no other choice, but they needed to know. I knew my parents would eventually come to terms with what had actually happened to me. They would be there with me to help me recover when no one else was. They had been there from an early age: watching my stolen kisses, managing my first heartbreak, and, in my case, helping me overcome the time in my life when I thought I was nothing. They still loved me, and their love was enough to give me the courage to push on. Love conquers all.

6
PEER PRESSURE AND PARTYING

I've never been much of a party animal. Then again, I wasn't invited to parties to begin with. High school is usually the first time that many of us are exposed to partying as a lifestyle rather than just attending get-togethers to celebrate birthdays or marathon movies. What's the difference between a party as a get-together and parties as a lifestyle? Well, for starters, a high-school party that's designed to be a *banger* will usually consist of an impromptu get-together when someone's parents are out of town and typically involves drinking and sometimes drugs. For those of you unfamiliar with the term "banger," a banger is a party—a total "rager," if you will.

I remember hearing stories in homeroom about what parties would take place over the weekend. Someone would say, "So-and-so is throwing a banger," and then girls would create a little sharing circle as they made rules about who could hook up with whom and who was off limits because they were dating this person or that or were attempting to get with them for the night. But I was always the odd man out, sitting attentively and hoping that, one day, I'd be invited to a banger too. I figured that maybe I would be if I paid attention to these conversations long enough. It's not that I wanted to actually go to a party; I just wanted to feel included with the group of girls. Instead, I sat there week after week, listening to my peers plan their outfits and their methods of transportation to and from the house and wondering why I was never invited.

High-school parties sort everyone into their designated rung on the popularity ladder. Though it's ridiculous when you think about it, high school really does thrive on stereotypes. Everyone is so concerned with finding their identity and niche that we label ourselves and one another as quickly as possible: cool, nerd, weird, whatever. From what I've seen of the professional world, that part of life doesn't change all that much after high school. It's quite a brutal awakening. The parties are typically by invitation only, and if you're lucky enough to be invited, chances are you're in the cool crowd. The highly overrated invites are saved solely for the people who've achieved popular status, which usually just means they're either jocks or hot girls who put out.

Hence the reason I was never invited.

Don't get me wrong; I was happy with who I was. At the same time, however, I desperately wanted to be included in what everyone else was doing. You know what I'm talking about. On the surface, you smile and say you don't care, but on the inside, you want to be included so badly that tears may sting your eyes later. My freshman year of high school, I was almost completely shunned from the party crowd. I was seen as a nerd. I never spoke to the popular kids, and they certainly didn't speak to me. I was fine with all that. Nothing much changed in my sophomore year. The only way I heard about what went on over the weekends was through the social grapevine. But when my junior year came around, that all changed.

Junior year, I was "seeing" a popular kid who was notorious for throwing the *best* high-school parties. We didn't have an official label, but everyone knew we were a "thing." He made me feel like I belonged. I hung out with the cool kids and didn't give two shits about what test I had that day because I was super cool. I was with Mr. Cool for three months; then that was the end of that. But during those three months, I was invited to parties.

The first party I went to was in my neighborhood, walking distance from my house. I'd invited my best friend at the time to go with me. She hated parties more than I did, and she cried the entire time we were walking to the house. She told me she felt like a whore wearing my tiny spandex skirt and a crop top, but I personally thought we looked good. We were two total babes going to our first high-school party . . .

looking like total prostitutes. In that moment, however, I didn't care. I felt honored that I had finally been invited to a party and immediately lost sight of my hatred for these events. I ignored my best friend as we walked to the house despite her constant pleas to go back home.

When we got to the party, there was a bouncer waiting for us at the door. The kids in my town were a little bit wealthier than most and wanted nothing more than to be like adults, so they did everything they could to create an exclusive, club-like party environment—hence the bouncer. He was a big Hispanic man who was checking names off a list. I couldn't believe it: here was an actual, physical representation of the infamous "Popular" list. And, for the first time ever, my name was on that list. We entered the luxurious home and were greeted by keg stands, red solo cups, and my peers, who were all drunk. Oh, and my "boy-thing" . . . who was completely plastered. My friend and I hung out for what felt like an hour, but in reality, we left after five minutes.

My first and only high-school party was horrific—all five minutes of it. I experienced firsthand how drinking and drugs could completely alter a person's life and morals, and I saw how worthless my boy-things's values were. He had been "cheating" (even though we were never official) and proceeded to do so right in front of me. He grabbed some drunken girl standing close to him and shoved his tongue down her throat. I approached him as soon as I saw this, and that was the end of our "thing," or whatever that relationship was. The following day, he called me like nothing was wrong; he thought we were still something.

The idiot had been too drunk the night before to remember what had happened. I had no problem calling him one last time, but I haven't spoken to him since.

From that moment on, I no longer wished to go to these parties, even if they meant being included. I decided that I didn't want to support the things parties like that did to people or the things drinking and drugs made people do—or allowed them to do. The sad part was that most of the people there didn't even remember the party the next day because they'd been so drunk. I didn't care if my peers thought I was popular or just another loser. I truly feel bad for the people whose names are on those lists. They did whatever they could to fit in and are now going to have to depend on alcohol and parties for self-completion, self-worth, and self-confidence. I think that's more pathetic than not getting invited to a party in the first place.

Movies and TV shows put these raging bangers in a positive light, much like they do with sex. At the end of the day, I think the media just wants to show people having a good time, regardless of the consequences or the improbability of the event. It doesn't matter how young you are; they want us to believe that partying is a rite of passage to becoming an adult. They show young girls and boys going to parties, drinking, and not getting caught by parents or the police. But the media seems to leave out what actually happens at these parties. The movie *Project X* glorifies partying to a new level, and I would think it an absurd premise for a movie except that, through my career, I've been to a number of parties that seem just like it. There was one in particular that I attended in California that was by far the craziest banger I've ever been to.

The party was up in the Hollywood hills and seemed to include every little detail from *Project X*. There were blow-up sex dolls floating in the pool, half-naked people walking around and swimming in the water, and music so loud I couldn't hear my own thoughts. I spent most of my night watching people make fools of themselves.

As the party went on, I saw a girl who couldn't have been three years older than me pass out in her own vomit. For a moment, I thought she was dead. Her so-called "friends" posed next to her for staged pictures, probably to post on social media. I couldn't believe my eyes. I was really concerned for the girl, but I had no idea what to do. I remember looking in her direction every so often to make sure she was okay. I've heard horror stories of young people choking on their own vomit; thankfully, she did not become one of them.

Once her safety was assured, I noticed another group of people having chicken fights in the pool and climbing on the support beams that held up the back of the house. The rest of the kids were taking shots off each other's bodies and diving into the highly occupied pool. Why? I still don't know.

Like I said, I hate parties. The only reason I went to this party in particular was because I felt like I had to live up the California lifestyle. It was supposed to be a fun start to my much-awaited summer vacation with my family. The owner of the house seemed to be completely okay with what was going on in their home, which, again, was strange to me. As the night continued, the adults, who were also intoxicated, even participated in the stupid events by playing beer pong and dancing alongside the partygoers.

The first noise complaint came around 11 p.m. The owner of the house answered the door to find a neighbor angrily pointing toward the back of their house. He kindly apologized and said he would ask the deejay to turn the music down. The music was turned down somewhat for twenty minutes, but then it resumed its thumping volume. Around midnight, the neighbor showed up on their doorstep again, this time slightly more agitated. He demanded that the music be shut off or he would call the cops. Hesitantly, the owner obliged and told the deejay to turn the music off. However, that also didn't last. Thirty minutes later, the party was back on.

The party was a total rager. It was also the first time I ever ran from the cops. Around 1 a.m., there was the third and final noise complaint from the neighbors. Cops showed up and immediately shut the party down. That's when I found out there was marijuana in the house. The police could arrest anyone who had ingested the illegal substances. It was my first run-in with the cops, and my friend and I decided to run down the property to the foot of the hill behind the house and hang out there until the cops left. I hadn't drank or done any drugs, but when people run, I'd suggest you run too. Thankfully, no one was arrested, and the parents were not held responsible because everyone was of legal age at the party. Everyone except for my friend and myself—but the cops didn't exactly know we'd been there.

The cops asked the cooperative homeowners if they would open their house to allow partygoers to stay overnight, considering how drunk their guests were. They obliged, so everyone came back into the house to "sleep." I ended up sleeping on the couch with my friend because it was too late to be driving. We left early the next morning. I woke up smelling like pot even though I hadn't had any. I was greeted by the sight of approximately twenty bodies sprawled out on towels all the way to the door. There were burnt-out joints all over the floor, along with an array of chips and salsa, empty bottles, candy-bar wrappers, and chunks of throw-up on several of the unconscious guests. I decided that it would be best to get my belongings and call an Uber. After what felt like twenty minutes of carefully stepping over bodies, I was out the front door and on my way home. Everyone else at the party considered it a total success—aside from the cops showing up.

I haven't been to a "rager" since. I was really bothered by seeing so many people out of it, and I don't understand why someone would do that for fun. I don't drink. I never have, and even when I am of legal age, I probably won't. Alcohol is a poison. It tastes like garbage, and the body isn't meant to ingest it. Why do you think people pass out and throw up all over themselves? I don't see how that's supposed to be fun.

The Safe Lie

There may be nights when you find yourself in a strange or uncomfortable situation, like the one I was in at that party. I didn't enjoy being there, and I should have left. If you find yourself in a situation like that, or in a worse one, and need an excuse to get out of there, *lie*. Do it. An uncomfortable party, a dangerous situation, a threatening date—if you have that weird feeling in your stomach, like the one you get when you know you have done something bad, remove yourself from the situation in any way you can. Usually, the best way is something I call the Safe Lie.

What is a Safe Lie? A lie that you have in place long before it is necessary to have. I used to tell my mom that if I called her and asked if she'd gotten my red poster paper, that meant there was something wrong. Totally out there and quite random, but oddly enough, it hasn't failed me. You can use your phrase to alert whoever needs to be told that you need help. After you use your code word or whatnot, you then find an excuse to leave. It could be anything. Hopefully, the person you called will say something like, "Come home," or, "I need help with something." Speakerphone is a great thing in situations like this; that way, those who are around you know that you're not kidding.

The lie isn't foolproof, but it works for me. Worst comes to worst, just run.

The Safe Lie has helped me in the past, and I know it will help in the future. I advise you to use this technique only if you have to. A perfect time to use it would be if you were in a situation that you had to get out of or avoid at all cost. Your safety always comes first. If the situation is that bad, just call the police. There may be times when your life is at risk. Be smart. Always use your best judgment because your intuition may save your life at some point. I hope you never find yourself in such a situation, but life throws many curveballs. If you surround yourself with the right people, you should not find yourself in uncomfortable situations. For the times you do, here is how to pull off the Safe Lie:

1. Decide that this is an appropriate situation in which to use the Safe Lie.

2. Use your safe word or phrase to alert the other person that your lie is about to arise.

3. Make sure you have the *same story* as the person who is included in your lie.

4. Keep it short, sweet, and simple.

5. Don't get caught lying.

6. Leave the area as soon as possible, with no hesitation.

7. Call an authority figure if you need to.

8. Make sure you are in a safe place.

9. Tell whoever helped you with your lie that you are now out of harm's way.

I highly recommend using the Safe Lie if you ever find yourself in a sticky situation. I have used my safe word, "pink flamingo," multiple times. I use this to advise my friends that I am about to lie and need them to back me up. I have faked phone calls; I've said that I have homework, a late meeting, etc. The list is endless. Just make sure you are safe. Hopefully, that checklist will be able to help you in some way or another in the future. I know it has helped me a lot over the years.

Choosing Your Influences

My parents never left me alone much when I was growing up, so I seldom had access to the house without their presence. I wasn't a bad kid. I was the type of kid that parents *could* leave at home without the fear of an extravagant underage-drinking fest taking place. My parents raised me differently, and I have them to thank for who I am. Sure, I was never left with the chance to throw parties of my own, but I know myself; had I been left alone, a party would have been the last thing on my mind.

I find myself believing that neglectful parents are the reason kids turn to drinking. The parents don't care, and therefore, their kids don't either. I've known parents who allowed parties at their house even in their absence. They usually supplied the alcohol but demanded that their kids' friends spend the night. There are other parents who even go so far as to rent out a house for their kids to crash in. Those parents believe that "kids will be kids," and kids will make mistakes, so they'd rather their kids do it in the house than on the streets. They make excuses for their kids. What kind of example are they setting in regards to authority and responsibility? I will never fully understand it.

The behaviors of those around you—whether they're your parents, friends, or peers—will begin to shape your character. They can encourage you correctly, become your demise, or drag you down with them. When certain behavior is broken down, it's peer pressure, plain and simple. We do what we observe: monkey see, monkey do. Those we surround ourselves with can encourage us to follow the right path, or they can hold us back from finding our full potential.

When we're kids, we conform to our peers to feel like we're accepted. I went to a high-school party that I knew I wouldn't like only because I wanted to be accepted by my new friends. As I've seen while working different jobs, adults will conform to other's standards for the sake of ease and power. Soon enough, we believe that things like drugs, friends, relationships, sex, and money will come easily if only we do as everyone else is doing. And maybe they will. But something I've learned is that if a thing is easy to accomplish, it's probably not going to last. If your friends don't push you to be better, do better, and reach higher, then whatever gratification you get from them in the moment won't satisfy you in the long term.

People will do almost anything to fit in. No one wants to be the outcast. We ignore or tease some people and clamor to spend time with those we deem important, all to feel important ourselves. Deep down, everyone wants to be wanted. People will do anything in order to feel that way. This is the reason peer pressure is such a pressing issue. We play follow-the-leader, and sometimes we follow the wrong person. Society tells us we have to fit a certain mold, so we try our best to please everyone around us—parents, friends, bosses, or partners— even if it requires us to step outside our morals. To make dumb choices like sleeping around, drinking, doing drugs, sneaking out, or going to stupid parties. When we're trying to gain acceptance, in the moment, the benefits seem to outweigh the costs.

I recently attended a meeting with some of the most successful businessmen in the amusement park industry. My dad had to go, so I tagged along. He told me to listen closely because I could learn something of value from the meeting. As I sat at the table with my father next to me, one of the men suddenly addressed a topic I was surprised to hear at a meeting like this. He started talking about his past and current acquaintances in business and his personal life. I sat there wondering where he was going with this. Was he facing problems he wanted to discuss with the men at the meeting? Was he lonely because of his career? He ended his speech by posing a question to himself, asking, "What would I have done differently as a young adult in order to be more successful?"

As the meeting continued, others began to chime in. Their comments sounded identical: "I'd choose the people I surround myself with more wisely." That day, I heard this over and over again. To become successful, one must surround oneself with motivated and successful people. Now, this doesn't mean you can only be friends with people who have a career, have money, and are going places, because those things aren't vital. What they did want to get across to me is that you should choose the people around you carefully because they can either help you or hurt you. At the time, I didn't know this conversation would begin to aid me in my own future endeavors.

What does all of this have to do with partying, you ask?

If you buy into the lie that parties are the only way to find acceptance and friends—if you give into the peer pressure to try to look cool by doing these things—you set yourself up for falling into the same pattern in college and beyond. I'm not saying that partying in high school will ruin your life. I'm saying that once you invite that kind of indulgence into your life, it's hard to break the habit. Before you know it, you could become that parent who rents a party house for your kid (who isn't old enough to drink) because you "were young once and remember how it felt."

My dad knows plenty of people from high school who partied and never left that stage in their life. I'm only eighteen, and I've already started to see parties become the demise of my peers. I have seen some of them get arrested, become pregnant, overdose, or even die in horrible wrecks. It is a sad day when you learn you will never see one of your classmates again. I cannot imagine the pain their families have had to feel because they allowed their kid to go out to just "be a kid" for the night. Little did they know that their child would never return.

There was a point in my life when I thought partying would help me become popular. I was tired of being an outcast. I wanted someone to invite me to one of those stereotypical high-school parties so I could feel like a popular kid just for the night. I thought that was the only way to secure friends and maintain a status of popularity. In reality, I could not have been more wrong.

The bitter truth is that a lot of the so-called popular kids turn out to be the biggest losers in the long run. They are the people who feel the need to become plastered and sleep around just to fit in. Imagine what they will be like in the years to come. It's become a trope in movies: the popular party guy in high school who now works at the local movie rental. People wouldn't keep creating these characters if they didn't all know someone just like that in real life.

The cycle, however, can become worse. The party types will come of legal drinking age, and they will more than likely be inclined to party even more because there are fewer consequences. But now the thrill of illicit partying is gone, so they think partying harder and longer will fill that "cool" void. If you party too much, you can lose your job, your friends, and you family. You may become someone who no one will want to have in his or her life, and the drinking and drugs will become your only form of release. There is a difference between having fun and being flat-out stupid. The choices we make as teenagers affect who we can become for the rest of our lives. I promise that there is no amount of popularity that you can receive in four years of your life that will make you a better person long term. I know that I can make something out of myself without having to put my name on a "Popular" list in order to do so. And so can you.

#BeenThere

When I met my now-husband in high school, he nicknamed me the "ice princess" because I struggled with being honest about my feelings. At first, it was just a cute nickname, but the more we used it, the more we realized how unhealthy my ice-princess tendencies were.

In talking with him about it, I realized my issues stemmed from my previous relationship. I had dated a guy a couple years before who had just absolutely smothered me. One day, we had an argument on our way to class. We had been holding hands, and after our fight, I let go of his hand and stuffed mine into my pockets. He grabbed my arm, wrenched my hand out of my coat, and held on to it tightly, forcing me to hold his hand even though I had made it clear I didn't want to. I was so mad at him, but I went quiet and kept walking, my hand hanging limply in his. In computer class, he would come up and try to kiss me while I was working. I told him once that it made me uncomfortable, but he kept on, so I stopped complaining and just let him do whatever. These small, seemingly harmless concessions ultimately led to me compromising my own needs for his sake. I often found myself feeling like a zombie, moving mindlessly through the motions of being his girlfriend. And I didn't end our relationship by being strong or honest or brave. My family moved out of state, and he ended it a few weeks later because of the distance.

Sometimes I reflect on that time and wonder why I let him treat me that way, especially now that I'm an outspoken person who can easily vocalize what I want and need. I can't really think of a reason except that I felt bad for him. He lived with his mom and his abusive stepdad, so I think my sympathy for him overpowered my self-empathy. But those many months of self-neglect created in me a habit of pushing away my own needs, of silencing my voice before it even had the chance to make a sound.

Fortunately for me, I met someone who pointed out the danger in my behavior, but it was such a part of me by then that it was a massive struggle to change. It almost broke our relationship; worse, it almost broke me. Thank God I found my voice before it was too late. Now I speak clearly and boldly. The ice princess is gone.

—Misty Bourne,

editor, age thirty-one

7
DRUGS AND ADDICTIONS

When I hear the word "drugs," I think of an immediate escape. But life doesn't work that way. There's no such thing as an immediate escape, but the scary thing about drugs is that they can make you feel like there is. They have the power to take away your problems for a moment while they quietly destroy your body and mind. Once your moment of "serenity" ends, you want it back, so you continue to pop pills, snort powder, or inhale smoke. A one-time experiment never really ends.

The saying "people will either want to be you, kill you, or kiss you" holds true in every interaction we have. People come into our lives as a blessing or to teach us a lesson. I once befriended a classmate whom I thought amazing at first. He had been one of my closest friends for quite some time, and he was someone I could trust, so we started dating. I knew from all of our conversations that his home life was not the best. His parents were divorced, and his mom struggled as a single parent. He ended up moving to another school in Central Florida. I noticed right away that he made friends with the wrong people.

He once told me how stoned he got after school. It broke my heart, and I told him that I wanted nothing to do with him if he did that again. But bad habits are hard to break. He assured me for over a year that he would never smoke again, so I reluctantly believed him.

One day, I ran into him late at night while I was walking my dog in my neighborhood. I smelled the distinct scent of weed on him. I confronted him immediately and, having given him a warning in the past, decided to break up with him. Over a two-day period, his newly found "friends" tried to convince me that it hadn't been him smoking. He had just happened to be around people who'd been doing drugs. Because I wanted it to be true, I believed them.

Clearly his friends were turning him into someone he wasn't. I still thought he was a good person, but I guess I was wrong. Now, he's in too deep with the wrong crowd, and it's consumed him. The saddest part is not that we are no longer friends but that he lost control of himself so completely. As I stated earlier, you are the people you hang out with. It's horrifying to see how those we surround ourselves with can influence who we are and who we will become.

I would like to believe that he thought they were good people. Sure, his life was hard, but it leaves me to wonder: Did I ever really know him? Maybe he was into drugs before our friendship began and I never knew. Maybe I was just gullible to believe his promises. At the end of the day, however, I don't know how he looks his mother in the face and lies to her. His mother is a wonderful woman who, all by herself, has tried to give him the world, and yet she has no idea what's going on. I know it isn't my place to step in, but I hate seeing how many kids lie to their parents because they have succumbed to peer pressure.

Teenagers, kids, and even adults like to believe that they are invincible, but really, they are not. We would all like to believe that we are smart when it comes to letting people into our lives. But how much do we really know about the people closest to us? What do they do in their own time, and how do they treat others? If you can answer that, think again, because chances are that you are wrong. I'd suggest talking openly with your friends to make sure you do really know them.

Prescription Drugs

Substances are tricky because everyone reacts differently to them. Sure, some people can handle some drugs better than others, but you can't know if you're one of those people without putting yourself at immense risk. Some people experiment once and die. I have been told that my body could handle certain types of drugs and that I would feel great. I always said no. No matter who we are and where we live, we all have access to drugs, both good and bad. These drugs can be anything from over-the-counter remedies in your parents' medicine cabinet to illegal substances people sell in your town.

When I was a kid, I loved cough syrup. I love it even now as a teenager. Cough syrup tastes like straight candy. Every time my mother gave me the syrup, my throat felt better and I became weary. Thus, I felt the immediate need to nap, and who doesn't love a good nap? There were days I'd pretend to be sick just to be given this tasty syrup. Then I'd just curl up and take a deliciously relaxing nap.

However, there were times even when I was neither sick nor faking sick that I felt the need to drink the cough syrup. I wanted to fall asleep quickly, and the syrup accomplished that. I'd sneak into the medicine cabinet late at night and take a sip. My parents began to notice that that cough syrup was disappearing. They began to hide it and told me we had run out. But for some reason, I craved this sugary substance. I felt I couldn't fall asleep without it. I had no idea I had gained a craving for the medicine and was forming an addiction. I had no idea what was in it or what it could do to me if I consumed too much.

There's a long list of seemingly harmless over-the-counter drugs. Prescription drugs range from cough syrups to sleep aids, painkillers, and more. All of these prescriptions seem harmless, but they can kill if consumed in large amounts. Here's the thing, though: over-the-counter drugs aren't hard to get ahold of. It's easy to abuse this type of drug because they're so easy to find. According to the National Institute on Drug Abuse (NIDA), part of the National Institutes of Health, US Department of Health and Human Services, twelve reasons teens are using prescription drugs are:

- 62 percent of teens say prescription drugs are easy to get from their parents' medicine cabinets.
- 52 percent say they're available everywhere.
- 51 percent say they're not illegal drugs.
- 50 percent say they're easy to get through other people's prescriptions.
- 49 percent say they can claim to have a prescription if caught.
- 43 percent say they're cheap.
- 35 percent say they're safer to use than illegal drugs.
- 33 percent say there's less shame attached to using them.
- 32 percent say they're easy to purchase over the Internet.
- 32 percent say there are fewer side effects than with using street drugs.
- 25 percent say they can be used as study aids.
- 21 percent say parents don't care as much if they're caught using them.

Here's where teens are obtaining their prescription drugs:

- 0.3 percent: bought on the Internet.

- 1.9 percent: from more than one doctor.

- 2.2 percent: other.

- 3.9 percent: from a drug dealer or stranger.

- 16.6 percent bought or taken from a friend or relative.

- 18.1 percent: from one doctor.

- 54.2 percent: *free* from a friend or relative.[4]

I remember when a police officer came to the high school I attended to give a seminar on drugs. At the time, I thought it was a joke. He stood in front of the entire student body and spoke about the seriousness of drugs both prescription and illegal. I remember making faces at my peers around the room and paying little attention to almost anything the officer said. I want to believe that I chose to tune him out because I never thought anything like that would happen to me or someone I knew. I'd never done drugs or had any interest in doing so, so why pay attention? I thought this until he spoke about statistics.

He turned on a PowerPoint and made us watch a video about a student from another school. He then went on to say that there had been more than twenty-five thousand deaths in 2014 alone due to prescription drugs—and the number was rising. This got my attention because that was twenty-five thousand young lives that would never have the chance to grow old. Twenty-five thousand people who died because they never thought they would be victims. I've learned that we think we're invincible, especially as young adults, but we really aren't. We tend to forget that we could overdose on drugs even if they weren't illegal. We could become a statistic, and I think we overlook that. I know I have.

Illegal Drugs

However, not all drugs can be bought over the counter. Some substances must come from a friend of a friend or from someone on a street corner. Illegal drugs have always been popular when it comes to pop culture and fitting in with the status quo. We look up to our favorite celebrities, and they pose with weed, cocaine, molly, etc. Super cool, right? I know these celebrities make these things look glamorous and free of consequences, but that's not the case. Snorting cocaine, smoking pot, or doing molly won't make you any more like a celebrity. You won't be revered, no one will worship you, and, in the long run, you'll only be harming your body. Who cares about that one moment when you'll feel cool saying yes given that you could spend a lifetime regretting that decision? Is it realistic for me to tell you to avoid any situation in which drugs are present? Probably not. But it is certainly realistic to expect that you can and will keep your distance from the drugs.

The entertainment industry avidly worships pot. I can say this because I see it more often than not. I see it often at social events, but the night I consumed it was by accident. I was at a party in good ole California with some fellow actors, and there was pot—a lot of pot.

However, I didn't know it was pot. Given the fact I was at a party, I thought it was just your typical party food: candy, brownies, and cake. In a sense, it was. Then again, it really wasn't.

I had been bouncing from audition to audition all day and felt I could really use a brownie (or a few). I plopped down on the couch in the corner as my friends were getting a drink from the craft table. I typically don't eat brownies—or multiple brownies, to say the least—so I decided to slam them down before anyone else knew.

My good friend came over and sat down next to me with her fruit punch cocktail. Her expression mimicked absolute horror. I honest to God remember only that look when I ask about that night; it was my last clear thought. She analyzed the crumbly chocolate evidence on my face and, with panic in her eyes, said to me, "How many of those did you eat?" At this point, I was still in denial of eating the brownies—but for the record, I'd had three.

She suddenly grabbed my wrist and ran over to our other friend. We immediately left the party. Little did I know at the time that my other friend, the one who hadn't seen the evidence on my face, was also high. The Uber ride back to the apartment was something else. I'd never laughed so hard in my entire life. For the first few minutes as the brownies hit me, I giggled to myself and stroked my friend's face. I even asked our Uber driver if he could stop at Pinkberry. I needed a yogurt desperately. I had the munchies fairly bad. To my good fortune, I decided on yogurt over potato chips. Our Uber driver was a genuine man who agreed to stop because he could see my friend was struggling to control me.

After I slammed down my yogurt, I moved into a stage of paranoia. Granted, we'd made it back to the apartment by this time. I'm told I sat on the couch, rocking back and forth. When this part of my reaction ended, I felt a creative burst of energy, and I apparently spitballed screenplay ideas to my friends. I think they were great ideas, and I wish I'd written them down. I can see why this drug is so popular in the entertainment industry because it really allows one to be creative. Yet after my creative burst of energy ended, I felt more paranoid, and I immediately passed out.

When I woke up the next morning in the same outfit as the night before, I realized I must have done something stupid. I not only smelled like pot (more than likely the result of secondhand smoke) but had bloodshot eyes. My good friend was already awake just to give me eyedrops and check my stability. Concerned, she told me that one brownie makes someone high and that I'd consumed three. You could say I'd had a lot of marijuana that night.

To this day, I have never again eaten something without asking what it was, never smoked a bong, and never gone to a party for drinks. I was high once, and that was enough. I know how common it is for entertainers to smoke pot; it relaxes you and takes the edge off. However, not everyone reacts the same way. I wasn't calm; I was paranoid. I did have a creative energy burst, but I am creative without the help of drugs.

Marijuana is a controversial drug that's been legalized in certain states. On the positive side, it has been known to stop seizures and take pain away from people who are suffering. I have nothing against marijuana in general, and I understand that some of my favorite artists could not live without it. However, I can say from experience that I don't intend on ingesting it again. I don't feel the need to take drugs to be successful in my career. That is the problem with drugs: we can become dependent on them, thinking they're the key to success in creative fields. Marijuana is a creative tool, but it won't necessarily lead to success.

My dad drove to my friend's apartment that morning to pick me up. Because we tell each other everything, I immediately confessed to him what had happened. I was surprised when his immediate response was laughter. He had always hated drugs and told me why I should never do them. Yet he still laughed. My dad always said that those who party and do drugs in high school wouldn't leave their hometown, and he was right: most kids who wasted their life being high or passed out drunk every night never got out into the world to work. The majority of those people are still washed up without a pot to piss in (as he would say). Not to mention that drugs can cut your life in half.

I can understand if you're at the point in your life at which you don't care about anything. I can understand your desire to escape. However, I can promise you that life will get better in the long run. If you turn to illegal substances, I wouldn't expect the outcome to be good. It will more than likely make things worse. I have seen people our own age go through hell because they got high one too many times or got caught selling contraband. One bad decision can have dire effects on your health and can irreparably derail your life.

One doesn't have to be an entertainer to get sucked into doing or selling drugs. The high school I attended is well respected globally and in our community, but the kids who attend mostly have wealthy parents. These kids often become bored, and use their parents' money to buy and sell drugs. I've personally witnessed people my own age get expelled from a prestigious school for selling drugs to other students. Teachers and faculty aren't as out of the loop as they may seem. They know what high schoolers are capable of, and I am sure they're sad to see their students caught up in drugs.

Just Say No

The entertainment industry has taught me a lot thus far when it comes to the use of narcotics. I spend a lot of my time in New York City, given that that's where most of my work is. Before I lived in New York, I had no idea how common and easily obtained illegal substances are. I've seen girls my own age carry around plastic bags full of a white powder. I first encountered these white bags when I was fifteen years old. It was strange. I always thought to myself, "Why would these models carry flour with them everywhere?" So one day, I decided to ask what exactly was in the baggie.

The girl looked at me, almost confused, and said, "Coke." Again, I had never been exposed to drugs like this, and I didn't know what "coke" was. When she figured out that I'd never been exposed to coke before, she took it upon herself to offer me some. I didn't know how cocaine was even ingested, and after my experience with pot, I thought you ate it. However, that's not how you do it; you either snort it or inject it with a needle.

When I hear the word cocaine, I now immediately think of the movie *The Wolf of Wall Street*. I became friends with a girl from the movie who had played one of Leonardo DiCaprio's character's prostitutes. I've noticed that there seems to be a blurred line between some characters and the actors that play them. I reference this movie because it not only illustrates how common drug abuse is among the wealthy but is also a great teaching aid. Of course, to some, it would be a dream to have endless money and hookers, but the drugs will take their toll on you after awhile. More than likely, the cops will come after you, and since drugs are illegal, you'll go to jail—no matter how rich you are. Sorry, but being wealthy doesn't mean you're above the law.

As I walk the streets of New York City, I often see an uncanny amount of homeless people. Most of the homeless here are drug users; some openly ask for drug money. I've been chased by a few who demanded I give them money for drugs and others who looked like they were not in control of their bodies. There is one particular homeless man I often see who pushes a cart between 7th and W57th Streets. As I was leaving the bank with my mother, we heard his daily ramble about how the government was out to get us all. I've never made eye contact with this man before except for on this specific day. I looked up, and he was standing right in front of me. He proceeded to scream, ". . . And it's all your fault, you crazy, Polish bitch!" He then chased my mom and me for two blocks until a nice NYPD officer came to our aid.

From that day on, I've often wondered about that man. I wonder how he ended up on the street corner and why he chases random people. Maybe he wants to run from his own life, since he must have made bad decisions to end up where he is now. It's sad to think how drugs can affect someone's life to this degree. Some homeless people are mentally handicapped, down on their luck, or just drug users. However, when all you have is nothing, what do you have to lose?

There will come a time in your life when you're offered drugs. Maybe you'll accept, or maybe you won't. However, keep in mind that every choice you make has a consequence and a benefit. The consequence could be death; the benefit could be a learning experience. Drugs aren't meant to be recreational, yet they seem to be.

The next time a cop comes to your school and talks to you about the seriousness of drugs, listen. You may not be the one who is abusing substances, but if you know someone who is, look out for them. The person you are now will mold who you will become for the rest of your life. My own experiences around narcotics have showed me that I am not missing anything if I don't get high. I am in control of my body and successful without the help of illegal substances. I understand that by sharing my own experiences with drugs, questions or assumptions about me may come up. I am okay with that. I've done drugs once, by accident, and that is the truth. One accident has caused me to take a stance against drugs and help others understand that they are not alone.

From this moment forward, I know that drugs will never disappear, and they will more than likely be offered to me within the next few weeks. I know that I will say no. I've learned how to say to no. Quite frankly, when you say no, people tend to respect you more. Those people may even wish they could have said no when drugs were offered to them. Just say no. I promise you that no high is worth your life.

Addiction

Addiction is a serious topic, and it is more common than we realize. Our lives are systematic, recurring, and routine; the main component that defines a routine is consistency, which can be good or bad. Addictions are a form of routine. After you form an addiction, accidents happen, relationships are lost, and you begin to retreat into yourself. You reach a point at which you believe that the only escape is succumbing to your addiction. At this point, you need help—medical help.

I realize you may refuse to admit that you have an addiction if you do have one. My words may not make you own up to your inner demons, but you know exactly what I'm talking about. You may or may not have something on your mind. Yet chances are you do. Whether it's drugs, sex, an eating disorder, or maybe biting your nails—it's an addiction. Addictions can alter your life and can be hard to break.

I, myself, have worked to overcome addictions. I was addicted to perfection; I wanted to be perfect. I never was, but I always strived to be. I ate healthy food and worked out all the time but still had some fat I could not seem to lose. That's when I realized that, in order to attain the perfect physique, I could make myself throw up after eating foods that I shouldn't have devoured. This was the start of my addiction—my own downfall. I talk about bulimia in more depth in chapter 9, "Health."

Addictions can be anything from a bad habit to a medical problem. From the time I have lived in New York City alone, I have seen some horrible results of addiction, especially one occurrence in late September. I was standing alone one warm night in the Union Square subway station, waiting to catch my train home. Out of the corner of my eye, I saw a man lying on his back, convulsing. The man was screaming and thrashing on the ground. My heart started racing as I stood, stunned, and watched this man flail uncontrollably. As luck would have it, an EMT and his team happened to be nearby. They ran over to him and strung him up to a chair as he tried to fight them off. I stood like a deer in the headlights until my train approached the station. I then walked onto the train in a trance-like state, only to realize later on that the man had overdosed.

Addictions can be begin to overtake someone's life. I have witnessed that firsthand. I understand that the following list will not shed light on some of the more serious cases of addiction that society is plagued with, such as in my story from above. If you're looking to further explore serious addiction topics and medical advice, I'd suggest checking out a local library or talking to someone with knowledge in this field.

The Top Twenty Addictions

I came across the following list in conversation, and it begged my mind for further attention. In order to best explain some addictions, I thought I would add my own personal commentary on the subject. Here is a list that I have compiled from common knowledge and from conversations with my older friends detailing the top twenty addictions today.

1. **Drugs:** This one is pretty obvious, and it makes sense that it would hold the title for most common addiction. Drug addicts can either be addicted to prescription drugs or to illegal substances. Yet prescription drugs are just as dangerous as illegal drugs when not properly consumed.

2. **Food:** Who doesn't love food? I have no further comment on this one. Well, perhaps you should eat healthier meals instead of ones from fast-food chains. Don't make yourself sick or put yourself at risk of obesity by eating empty calories everyday. Fill your stomach up with nutrition, and

your body will thank you. Fun fact: America has the highest obesity rate of all countries in the world. On the other hand, if you work out as much as I do, you understand that you have to fuel yourself almost constantly. Clearly, this does not mean shoving sugar down your throat. The root of the problem here is that the foods that most Americans eat lack nutritional value—hence why we are the fattest nation.

3. **Shopping:** I understand that, as a teenager, you enjoy hanging out at the local mall. There is nothing wrong with that, as I find myself doing the same thing when I can, but spending money can become addictive.

4. **Gambling:** See, now this one, I don't quite understand. Gambling is basically risking your *own* money in hopes of winning more money. Seems like a 50/50 shot. Regardless, it's a horrible risk to partake in and teenagers aren't old enough to gamble. This addiction is looking at you, adults.

5. **Love:** There is a song called "Addicted to Love," originally by Robert Palmer and recently covered by Florence and the Machine, that I believe was onto something genius before this list even surfaced. I've heard of sex addicts, and though I'm not personally acquainted with the subject, it would surely be an interesting topic to understand. Some people, however, love the thought of being in love regardless of the

person they choose to be with, as long as they are, in fact, "loved." This type of people loves being in love. Strange, if you ask me.

6. **Exercise:** I won't lie; I find myself guilty of this. I exercise way too much. I enjoy it, but I've found that when I don't go to the gym, I feel horrible. I feel that I have wasted my entire day if I don't go. I am sure some of you "meatheads" can relate to that.

7. **Work:** The never-ending quest for wealth or financial stability. Luckily for us teenagers, we are usually only exposed to part-time jobs at this age. But lo and behold what we have to look forward to.

8. **Internet:** I can only imagine that number eight is mainly an addiction of teenagers. The wonderful invention of the World Wide Web has created electronic monsters: people who spend way too much time on the Internet, to the point that when they can't be online, they feel they're missing out on life. I think we rely too much on the screen to see what other people are doing. In a way, we've become almost like stalkers—always looking out for a new meme, post, tweet, or snap. But the reality is that while we're watching other people's lives through the screen, we're wasting our own.

9. **Pornography:** People will deny whether they watch porn or not. I don't have anything further on this subject.

10. **Lying:** Pathological lying? This is yet another topic to which most teenagers can relate.

11. **Stealing:** I'd advise against this. You'll get caught. Do you really want to go to jail?

12. **Arson:** I could only hope that this addiction is becoming less popular.

13. **Video games:** Also known as teenage heaven. This is the most relatable subject to teenagers as a whole. Whether with Candy Crush, the Xbox, the Wii, Playstation, etc., we all game.

14. **Money:** Yes, money can be a good thing. Money allows for a stable lifestyle, but too much can corrupt a soul.

15. **Fame:** An overrated aspiration is to live in the limelight. There's more to life than how many Instagram followers you have or how many "likes" your latest duck-face selfie got.

16. **Power:** I feel everyone is guilty of this. It makes sense; liking power shows that you like to be taken seriously. But there's no need to be all Christian Grey about it.

17. **Rage:** Just calm down. Try yoga.

18. **Body Image:** I suffer from this one as well; I'm sure we all do. You're perfect as you are. I'll discuss this more later.

19. **Adrenaline:** I think adrenaline is beautiful. It creates a moment of pure living, in which you realize that life doesn't

last forever. In that moment, you are truly experiencing—and truly appreciate—what it means to be alive. It's pretty great, not going to lie.

20. **Television:** Can we substitute for Netflix? I feel Netflix is just as guilty, possibly even more so. Television is so mainstream.

My Addictions

I'm going to break the awkward ice of admitting that I have addictions too. My addictions are not life altering, nor do they call for medical attention. However, they do affect my everyday life. Everyone has some type of addiction. Please don't go into denial because you obsess over something. We all do. Addictions become serious when they affect your daily ability to function properly. I will flat-out name my addictions that most commonly affect my ability to function on a daily basis so that you feel better about addressing yours.

1. **Coffee:** I can never have too much coffee. Coffee is my own personal drug. I get withdrawal headaches when I don't have at least two cups. I become angry; imagine a little female Hulk on a never-ending conquest for coffee. Why is coffee so addicting? It has caffeine. Caffeine, believe it or not, is a drug. Caffeine can be found in soda, coffee, tea, etc. When it's consumed in large amounts, it

becomes addicting. If you, like me, try to go completely cold turkey when it comes to your caffeine intake, you will turn into a bitch for a while. Expect headaches, agitation, and constant aggression. I wouldn't recommend the cold-turkey approach. My advice is to slowly get that caffeine intake down to a safer number, such as one cup a day of any caffeinated beverage.

2. **Doing tasks in sets of two (OCD):** Ever since I was a kid, I've had to have two of everything—whether it be two kisses from my mom before I go to bed or two apples instead of one. Honestly, I have no idea what compels me to do this, but it has followed me ever since. This type of addiction is not life threatening, but it is a horrible habit I have somehow attained. Thankfully, it has died down in recent years, but it still resurfaces from time to time. I also have an underlying obsession with returning my knickknacks to a specific spot. Why? I am a control freak, also known as having OCD (obsessive–compulsive disorder). This is a disorder that is caused by anxiety. Now, anxiety and addiction are not quite the same. However, if I do not have my way when it comes to my OCD, I become extremely uneasy. As I've gotten older, my OCD has died down. To this day, I still have traces of OCD, but it's nothing worth seeking medical advice

over. I tell myself everything will be okay if things don't go directly as planned.

3. **Working:** I know it may seem weird, but do you know many other seventeen-year-olds who've written a book? I don't. I have always had the urge to be working, whether it be writing, cleaning, washing cars, babysitting, or pretty much anything else. I just enjoy keeping busy. Sure, many teenagers would rather sleep—but not me. Regardless of what day of the week it is, my mind will be in a book or doing something productive. Work is fun to me and always will be. There is a high chance that I have ADHD because I always have to be occupied with something, but I would not trade that for the world. However, if you work too much, your mind can become stressed, and that is also not good for the human body. Everything in moderation.

4. **Cell phone:** Admit it. You're addicted to your cell phone too. I check mine every few minutes even when it doesn't go off. It's quite a problem. We're slowly losing our verbal skills because we feel the need to shoot a text to the person sitting directly in front of us. Unfortunately, this will never go away unless you commit yourself to the separation of technology. At dinner, perhaps leave your phone in another room or in your bag. If you're out with your friends, pay

attention to them and not to your Twitter feed. Thanks for killing relationships, technology.

5. **Social Media:** I don't know about you, but I find myself on Twitter, Instagram, Facebook, and Snapchat quite often. I think there's something to be said about how narcissistic we've all become. I feel the obligation to post photos and videos with the world. To a degree, no one really cares about our personal lives as much as we hope they do, but I feel that social media has created some sort of self-sufficient worth. We create a following and feel the need to live up to impressing them. Social media has also become some weird channel for stalking. We like to creep on people we talk about and see what they're doing. For some odd reason, we then compare ourselves to them and try to outdo them. I have seen friendships and relationships end when one person likes someone else's photo. Seriously, is this what it has come to? Social media not only kills your battery and your social life but also takes time away from your life outside your screen.

Overcoming Addiction

If you have a minimal addiction, such as drinking too much coffee or running everyday, don't worry. We all suffer from things like that. I am sure you can overcome it by yourself in good time. It may just be a fad. But addictions that are hazardous to your health *need* and *demand* attention from an adult or from another parental figure who loves you.

But on a more serious note, you can tell I don't have any serious addictions such as drinking, partying, or drugs. Yet I turn on the television and see kids our age who have died from their addictions—very serious ones. I personally know people who have died because they drank too much or took the wrong drug (prescription or illegal). I have already talked about the seriousness of prescription drugs. They can be just as bad for you as illegal substances.

All jokes aside for a second here, addiction is a serious thing. Bad habits can easily become addictions. They usually start with the statement, "It will only be a one-time thing." Then that "one" time turns into ten. Boom. Addiction.

Now, I am not a doctor, nor do I claim to be. But my goal here is to offer advice, like we teenagers give one another. I want to help you get over your addiction, whether it's minimal or large. I need you to admit to it. Tell someone that you have a bad habit that disrupts your life or something that you believe you cannot live without. Speak up, *please*. We're just kids. I hate to admit it, but we do need guidance. I realize your parents will try to keep you grounded; I understand that you just want to live a little. However, if you form bad habits now, it will affect you later. If it's a Saturday night and you're craving alcohol or drugs . . . that's a problem. Why do you think you have to be twenty-one to purchase alcohol? It's addicting, as are other substances. As teenagers, we cannot handle addictions; we don't quite know when to stop. Sure, I may sound like a killjoy, but do you want to be dead in a casket? Do you want your family grieving over your death before you even reach adulthood? No; I know I sure don't.

So what I am asking from you, whether you listen to me or not, is to identify addictions within yourself before it's too late. This does not require you to change your life in a day; no one can. If you are facing a habit that you cannot seem to shake, talk to someone. It will become an addition if it's not taken care of. I do not mean your OCD or caffeine intake here. I am talking about serious addictions that can be hazardous to you or to those around you.

If you know someone who's struggling to overcome an addiction, offer your help as a friend. Everyone needs a friend or someone to talk to, but remember: you're not a doctor either. If you feel that someone's life may be in danger, please call the police. Don't wait. Seconds count when it comes to saving a life.

Addictions can end lives. Please don't ever let yourself or someone you care about become a statistic for teachers to read off during depressing seminars. You have so much potential. Your life is and will be what you make of it. You'll have to make choices, and yes, you will not always make the right ones, but that does not make you a bad person. You will learn from your mistakes. Learn how to say no. Learn how much is enough for you to handle when it comes to activities you participate in or to putting any type of substance in your body. You need to understand your body and your limits because no one else can tell you what is best for you. No one can force you to do anything you don't want to do. It's crucial to surround yourself with people who will look out for you, but in the end, you will be your biggest supporter. Take care of your body, and your body will take care of you.

#BeenThere

When I was fifteen, most of my friends started smoking pot. I tried it once and didn't really like it all that much, but it was such a big part of the culture of my friend group that I just went along with doing it as much as my friends did. At first, it was once in a while. Then it was every time we hung out. Then we would sometimes even sneak out of school for smoke breaks. After a while, I actually started to like it enough that I smoked it on my own, usually before bed or before watching movies alone. One night, my mom caught me smoking. The look in her eyes was enough to tell me how disappointed she was. She didn't even need to say the words. Instead of stopping with the pot, I continued; I just got better at hiding it. Eventually, things got worse and worse. My grades started slipping, and the friends who'd gotten me into smoking started doing harder drugs. It took about a year, but I finally decided to walk away from those friends. If I could go back, I'd tell myself to walk away way sooner. I lost so much of my high-school life to pot. I missed pep rallies, football games, and innocent dates to the movies with friends. No amount of pot was worth the time I'll never get back.

—Kelly McLaughlin,

teacher, age twenty-six

8
PARENTS

Mom and Dad:
I love you for forever, I like you for always,
As long as I'm living your for-real baby I'll be.
—adapted from Robert Munsch's *Love You Forever*

I remember the first time I told my parents, "I hate you." I don't remember why I said it, and even now, I can't imagine a valid excuse for such hateful words. I threatened my dad that when I turned eighteen, I would leave our house and never look back. I have been beyond cruel to my parents in the past. I've said things that I didn't mean, but my words still broke their hearts. I know we've all heard this before, but it's true: you can never take back the words you used to hurt someone. The saying "sticks and stones can break my bones, but words will never hurt me" is complete bullshit. I wish I could take back the harsh words I've said to people, but above all, I wish I could take back the things I've said to my parents. Saying sorry isn't a bad place to start.

My parents have always been there for me, ever since I popped out into this world. They have given me nothing but love and happiness, even if I haven't always returned the sentiment. I wouldn't be able to remember much of my early years without their dedication to creating and recording memories. They always had a camera and camcorder ready, documenting all the hand-holding, the nursery rhymes my mom sang, and the way my dad tossed me into the air like I was "Superbaby." They wanted me to remember and to see how strong their love has always been. Without all the photos, videos, and stories, I'm not sure how much of my childhood I would be able to remember as I grow older.

Part of being a teenager is trying to find yourself. We're most interested in having time to reflect, text, listen to music, or just do whatever makes us happy—without our parents bugging us. I think it's safe to say that being a teenager is tough on everyone. We're in a physical and mental limbo where we *look* mature but still having growing to do, and we *feel* mature but don't have the world skills or, frankly, the emotional caliber to survive on our own. I still flip-flop between feeling prepared for adulthood and feeling utterly unequipped. Though scary, it's also exciting. However, although these years are exciting for us, they can often be the hardest years on the people raising us: our parents.

My mom was the first person to say that I had an old soul. She used to tell me that I was her little grown-up. My dad, however, said he saw me really grow up after I started working, traveling, and dealing with subjects adults face. I felt more grown up, too. I was no longer the little girl that my mom and dad had brought into this world. I felt older, more mature, somehow. Looking back, I can admit that I've been strong-willed since a young age, but modeling convinced me that I knew what I was doing, even though I was still so young.

The first time I went to Miami to start modeling, I wanted to seem as grown up as possible. I was embarrassed when my mom or dad walked me in for some of my first jobs. I'd beg them to stay outside because I didn't want to seem like a kid. I would scream that I didn't need their help and slam the car door shut. I would even sometimes say that I didn't want them there and they should just leave. Only now do I realize how much that must have hurt my sweet and loving parents. They just wanted to be there for me and see their little girl succeed.

When we went to New York City for the first time, I did the same thing. I was so caught up in becoming a superstar that I neglected those who loved me most. I would leave them alone in the apartment when I went out with my new friends or when I got to meet my idols and even my parents' own idols. I wish I could go back and view my parents how I do now, but I can't, so I can only hope that they'll forgive me. Now, I always want them with me wherever I go. I've discovered we often push away the people whom we love the most, maybe because, deep down, we believe they'll always come back. This isn't always the case, of course, and I'm very lucky to have such patient and supportive parents. I pushed and pushed and pushed them, yet they still managed to love me.

I saw my mother break down when she began to realize how quickly I'd grown up. The three of us were visiting Florida State, my first choice for college. I was beyond happy to get to see the campus for the first time. College was still a year out for me, but they could see how much I wanted to go to that school. Everything was going fine at first when we arrived at Florida State. We went to Jimmy John's for lunch. My dad made a small joke about Mom having to sit in the back of the car when they dropped me off at college next year, and that was when Mom lost it. She broke down crying in the sub shop. As I tried to eat, I could not seem to enjoy my food. I didn't want to look at my mom as she bawled her eyes out. So instead, I sat there and cried too.

My mom is a very emotional person, and the older I get, the better I understand her. When I saw my mom break down in the restaurant, I realized that my future is closer now than ever before. The thought of leaving my parents makes me so sad, even though, not too long ago, I was counting the days. As I watched my dad hold my mom, I saw how strong he was. I know he wouldn't cry in front of my mom or me. He's able to hide his emotions much better than my mom. I've only seen him cry three times, and that is three more times than I ever would have liked to see. The first time was when he lost his dad; the second, when we cleaned out his childhood home; and finally, when my grandma was hurt, as I'll discuss later.

I can't imagine what it feels like to lose a parent. I dread that day very much. But my mother and father tell me not to think about it and to fill that void with love. My dad told me that his parents never showed much affection in their household, but he loved his father nonetheless. He told me that his dad was his own personal hero, and he hoped he could be mine too.

The truth is, my dad is my hero. Well, both my parents are. I've never been able to admit that before. I once would have said that my role model was some celebrity or someone out of reach, but I'd never say that now. Now I understand that my two heroes have been with me all along. They love me unconditionally and have given me every opportunity they could. They love me regardless of the dumb decisions I've made and will make. They have always been by my side, through the countless mistakes, heartbreaks, and harsh words. No intangible hero or idol could ever have given me half the support I was lucky enough to have from my parents.

Love from a parent or guardian is a type of unconditional love unlike any other. It never dies. At the end of the day, we can say almost anything to our parents, and they will always love us. It's been said that a parent's job is to love and not necessarily be loved. A parent should be a parent *and* a friend, not just a friend. I'm trying to learn as much as I can from my parents every day, because I'm running out of time in which I'll be living with their constant guidance.

Our parents are usually right, whether we like it or not. I know that, as a teenager, it can be hard to listen to opinions that we feel are "irrelevant." However, our parents do know what they're talking about.

They've seen their share of heartbreak, they've made some regrettable decisions, and they've discovered firsthand what it means to truly grow up. As much as we would like to think they are wrong about certain matters, they usually aren't. Deep down, I know that parents want us to make our own mistakes, as we should, but they also want to be the ones we turn to when things don't go as planned. Parents want us to love them just as much as they love us.

As I think about the future, I'm excited but timid. I know my parents enjoy watching me blossom into a young woman, but as I get older, so do they. Someday they won't be able to chase me around, go to early morning workouts with me, or travel as much as we do now. The thought of that makes me quite sad and brings tears to my eyes when I think about it too deeply.

I've previously overlooked the memories that my parents and I have made together because they are all I've ever known: the family vacations, the nights spent camping out under the stars, every birthday, every card, every meal. I think these things will last forever because, deep down, I still believe that my parents are invincible. Rationally, I know they're not, but it's a hard concept to wrap my mind around.

I know there will come a day when I won't be able to pick up the phone to hear their voice or drive in my car to go see them. There will come a day when I have to take care of them, just like they took care of me. I know they won't live forever, and neither will I. Then again, nothing on this earth lasts forever. Someday, I will be with my parents again for entirety, just how it's supposed to be.

Until then, I cherish every waking moment I can with them. My parents have made me who I am today, and I love them unconditionally. Never allow yourself to overlook the love from your parents, I can promise they love you more than you understand. They only want what is best for you—always. At one time, I didn't understand a parent's love, but the little things along the way helped me realize what truly matters. Though I was once a child eager to grow up, I can now say that I wish I could be young just a little longer to remain in my parents' loving arms forever and ever. When it seems like their main goal is to control every aspect of your life, remember: you're their little baby.

Hopefully, there will come a day when I'll become a parent, too. I know my parents look forward to that, even though it won't happen for a while. I know they want me to find my true love and get married. I just hope I can be as happy with my significant other as they are with one another. Until then, I'll do everything in my power to show my parents how much they mean to me. I will return the love they have given me for as long as we all exist and even afterward. My kids will know so much about their wonderful grandparents. When I have kids, I hope I can be even a fourth of the parent to them as my parents are to me.

#BeenThere

I was that kid in middle school who wasn't allowed to read *To Kill a Mockingbird* because of the swear words. Instead, I had to sit in the hallway during discussion time, doing worksheets on a different book and feeling alienated, sure that everybody in class thought I was the biggest dork in eighth grade.

So when I was introduced to *The Vagina Monologues*—a candid, funny, enlightening book about women, sexuality, health, and body image—in my senior year of high school, obviously my natural reaction was to hide it immediately upon bringing it home. It was unlike anything I had ever read. It was honest, open, and full of words that would've sent my parents into fits of hyperventilation.

But as I searched around my room for the best place to hide it, I realized it would be better for me to own up to it rather than act ashamed of something I didn't actually feel ashamed of. So I just put it in the stack of books on my bedside table, and that was that. A few days later, I went to read some more of it and realized it was missing. I knew immediately what had happened: my parents had found the book and had taken it. But why hadn't they approached me? Were they testing me to see if I'd come and talk to them about it? Maybe they didn't want to talk to me about it. Not shocking, after the *To Kill a Mockingbird* incident.

My parents meant well in trying to shelter me. I don't resent them for it. They made the best decisions they could . . . and so did I. I was not going to be like my parents. I wasn't going to pretend vaginas and controversial books didn't exist. I went to them and asked straight up, "Hey, why'd you take my book?" I don't really even remember the conversation that followed. The lesson wasn't in what they told me, because, honestly, they didn't tell me much—these things were better avoided than addressed. The lesson was in my owning my decision—in the value of education over ignorance.

—Misty Bourne,

editor, age thirty-one

9

HEALTH

We often hate our own bodies more than we hate our worst enemy. People will tell you things like, "You should love your body; you only have one," or, "You're beautiful the way you are," but you'll never listen. It sounds horrible, I know, but it's hard to look past our awkwardness and flaws, especially as teenagers, to see what other people are talking about. We've transitioned from carefree children who didn't worry about the complexities of life or what our bodies looked like to young adults who now have to deal with puberty—and all bets are off when we reach that point. We all put on weight and go through that so-called "fat stage." Some of us are able to quickly shed a few pounds and morph into a somewhat-better-looking person, while others take a little longer to blossom. We all hope to start our adult lives off with a banging body, but hope and genetics alone won't get us there—we've got to work for it.

Fitness is one of the most crucial aspects of your health. It will help you to escape that awkward teenage body in which you feel so entrapped, and you may even increase your own lifespan if you learn how to take care of yourself properly. There are two aspects of fitness: exercise and eating well.

I've learned that it's okay to enjoy your guilty pleasures in moderation. One chocolate chip cookie won't make you fat. It's perfectly okay to treat yourself every once in a while, but the old saying "You are what you eat" holds true. If you're eating mostly carbs and fats, your body will begin to reflect that. A lot of teenagers are still growing and have incredibly fast metabolisms, but this *will* catch up with you later in life, so you should start to eat consciously now.

That's part of the reason I don't rely on my own metabolism to keep me fit. It's possible that I chose to live a healthier lifestyle because of the career path I found myself on. When I was fourteen, I turned to an alternative style of eating with a strong workout schedule. I found myself eating few-to-no carbs and high amounts of protein, fruits, and veggies. Today, I still eat the same way. I cut out all the fatty foods from my life—not because I had to but because I wanted to.

Before I got introduced to the industry, I ate like a madman. When I got home from school, I would eat two chocolate-covered bananas, a quesadilla, some trail mix, and fruit. On the weekends, I would start my day off with a Coke Slurpee and a chocolate-glazed doughnut. I could eat pizza after pizza and steak after steak. I have always loved food, and I embrace it whenever it's offered. Now I just try to be more selective about the things I choose to eat.

The reason I'm telling you this isn't because I'm trying to end the obesity epidemic in the United States. I don't think that will happen in our lifetime. I'm not here to try to recruit you to join some hippie diet, either. I'm writing this because I want you to live a life you will enjoy. If eating burgers and ice cream every meal will make you happy, then go for it. No one's going to stop you. But be aware that these "pleasure foods" are made up of empty calories. They won't do anything to help you live longer; in fact, they may even begin to kill you slowly from the inside, if your body can't handle them. The pleasure you receive from them is temporary, but the damage they can do may last a lifetime.

My Struggle with Bulimia

If you're like many Americans, there may come a time when you need to lose weight for your own health. Do yourself a favor and go to a dietitian or nutritionist instead of trying to do it on your own. Starving yourself or eating only one Big Mac instead of two won't do the trick. A professional can help tailor a diet specifically for your body's needs, which will be the most effective and safest way to lose weight. I wish I could tell you that losing weight is easy, but it's not. Some people lose weight to become healthier, others because they feel compelled to fit an ideal of beauty, regardless of their health. I myself struggled with my weight for many years as I tried to be something impossible: perfect.

Most fashion models, who are anywhere between five feet eight to five feet eleven, weigh in from 118 to 125 pounds. No one cares about how much muscle you have or how young you are when it comes to these numbers. When I was fourteen, I was told I needed to weigh 125 pounds. I was about five feet ten at the time and 136 pounds, mostly muscle. I was happy with my body and had a healthy BMI. The only unhealthy thing about the situation was telling fourteen-year-old Makaila to lose eleven pounds in a month.

I was determined to lose the weight as soon as possible. I worked with trainer after trainer; I think I've worked with over five in as many years. They all claimed that they could help me lose weight quickly and safely. Well, that didn't work. They had me do almost every workout that was meant to slim down the body. I did cardio, Pilates, yoga, resistance training, interval training—all to get me "runway ready." At present, I weigh 131 pounds, so if I were to follow the industry's standards today, I would not be "runway ready" now. Fortunately, the agency I'm with now doesn't have a problem with this, and the types of jobs I submit for don't require me to fit that standard.

Aside from working out, I had to change my entire diet. I've tried pretty much every diet known to man. I started with the Atkins diet, then the no-carb diet, followed by juice cleanses, the cabbage-soup diet, the military diet, etc. From every trainer I worked with and every diet I tried, I learned the 80–20 Rule: eighty percent of getting the body you want is what you eat, while only twenty percent is actually working out.

So to get that twenty percent, I started going to gym. I would start my school days every morning by waking up at 4:45 a.m. to start my workout at LA Fitness by 5 a.m. I then worked out for two hours before homeroom started, and I was never late to school once. I busted my butt to lose eleven pounds in a little over a month, and I succeeded. I looked sick, but for some reason, I thought I looked perfect. I was told that skinny and sickly was perfect, so I believed it.

As my body began to develop, I found that it was difficult to stay at that size. Regardless of what I ate, or didn't eat, I put the weight back on. I continued to work out two or three times a day, but nothing seemed to work. I could not keep from gaining weight. I was still eating the same way I had before—fruits, veggies, and protein—but nothing seemed to do the trick.

In times of desperation, I resorted to something other models said was foolproof: the fastest way to lose weight was by throwing up. Before I got the contract with Wilhelmina and was told that, if I wanted to become a model, I would need to lose weight, I'd never made myself throw up. I hate vomit; it smells and is disgusting. Yet every time I ate something sugary or felt too full, I found myself on my knees over a toilet bowl. My finger plunged down my throat. I felt my throat burn as it tried desperately to push my finger back out. A stream of tears ran down my face, but my fingers remained where they were until my last meal splashed into the toilet.

One day, my parents sat me down on the couch. They had heard me gagging in my bathroom and told me they were going to get me help. As parents, they were forced to do something. I remember them taking me to dietitians. I hated the doctors because they told me that I needed to eat normally and that I wasn't healthy. Logically, I knew I wasn't healthy, but I didn't care, because I now looked the way I was told I needed to look in order to succeed. I was so blinded by the desire to meet those standards that I truly believed I was on the right path to being my best.

At the time, I thought something was wrong with me because I couldn't be as tiny as some of my heroes. I was infuriated every time anyone told me to "eat normally." I was so angry with myself for being a woman and going through puberty. I was mad that I was growing up and developing; I wanted it to stop. My parents persisted in getting me the help that I needed. Although you can heal physically, mental and emotional damage can't always be undone. My disorder still lingers to this day, appearing when I sometimes look in the mirror and think I'm not perfect. The truth of the matter is that no one's perfect. I'm not perfect, you're not perfect, and Victoria's

Secret models aren't perfect. We all have flaws, whether we choose to admit it or not.

Redefining Beauty

The media has altered the way we look at our bodies, no doubt about it. They have redefined society's ideal body image to something unhealthy and unattainable, and it's misleading and harming everyone. I see pictures of young girls starving themselves to have a thigh gap or abs or to wear a size zero. They're just children. The quest for a perfect body is destroying the innocent pleasures of childhood. It will never be okay to allow a job, a role model, or anyone else to tell you that you need to change into something you're not.

Photoshop has become the fashion industry's best friend. Girls are airbrushed, edited, and made perfect after the shoot. Ever notice how there are no flyaway hairs, lines, or weird colors in magazine photos? All thanks to Photoshop, transforming models from gorgeous to perfect.

When I went through my stage of bulimia, I was ashamed of myself. I had allowed others to tell me that I wasn't good enough. But who's the real culprit here? Society as a whole is to blame. We've worked ourselves up to believe that the human body's value lies in unobtainable aesthetics instead of natural functionality. Women are meant to have curves—we bear children, after all. And believe it or not, men also fall victim to body shaming. Men are supposed to be men, not some washboard for girls to fawn over. There's a fine line between true beauty and false advertising.

Your own health should be your top priority. I know that I would rather be happy in my own skin and embrace who I am than be unhappy and sickly. I thank God every day that I have my parents and friends to support me in even my roughest times. Bulimia didn't help me lose weight; it only messed my insides up. There are so many different types of eating disorders, such as binge eating and anorexia. It's easy to tell if you have an eating disorder if you're purging, vomiting, or hating yourself after you eat. Eating disorders are a serious subject and shouldn't be taken lightly. If you are reading this and struggle with your own body image, please consult a doctor or your parents. I know it can be hard—I've been there—but nothing is worse than being miserable about yourself. You're built the way you're supposed to be. Eat healthy, reward yourself every once in a while, and work out daily. Your body will thank you.

There is a campaign by Lane Bryant called #I'mNoAngel. When this campaign first hit the national markets in 2015, it sparked immediate controversy, especially since it was a direct attack against Victoria's Secret, which calls its supermodels "angels." The Lane Bryant campaign features beautiful plus-size women who show off their curves—a fashion industry no-no—and what true confidence looks like. True beauty comes in all shapes and sizes. The women in the #PlusIsEqual campaign all encompass something that your everyday fashion model sometimes lacks: self-acceptance, inner beauty, and positivity.

Both men and women should feel beautiful regardless of their size and shape. However, you only have one body, and you should still strive to keep it as healthy as possible. Don't conform your body to something you're not; instead, take care of the natural beauty you possess. Other beauty businesses, including Dove and Aerie for American Eagle Outfitters, have also begun to advocate for positive body images for all sizes. I pray that the Lane Bryant campaigns have a domino effect on the media and the way our society perceives the ideal body. If multimillion-dollar companies can love the body the way it should be loved, why can't we?

In order to change the way we view our bodies, maybe we should reconsider our role models. As a young girl, it's easy to be convinced that everyone should have a Victoria's Secret Model body. That's clearly not the case. I personally think those girls are absolutely beautiful, but part of what makes them so ideal is that their body shape is different from others: they're very tall and very lean. I'd love to become a Victoria's Secret Angel someday—that's always been my dream. I don't want this because of the fame; I want my story to climb up with me. I want to say that I succeeded at becoming a Victoria's Secret Angel *after* I beat bulimia.

Most people are not born looking like Amazonians, yet we fault each other for it. The fashion industry, as with the entertainment industry, is a brutal business in which your body is constantly scrutinized. There comes a time when you have to realize that it's not personal; it's just the way the industry works. But it's not as black and white as separating business from the personal lives of everyone else. The industry bleeds into the minds of young girls everywhere who aspire to be like their "ideal" role models. Sadly, those role models are often chosen for us by a panel of people analyzing every measurement.

If you aspire to be like your favorite model or actress, skinny and seemingly flawless, it's time to change role models. Look up to someone who is healthy and happy. Remind yourself every day that you are beautiful just the way you are and that everyone has their own flaws—they may just be better at hiding them.

Health is about more than just the food you eat. Health deals with everything you choose to do to your body. The choices you make when it comes to your body will, in some way or another, have a long-term effect on your life. I've learned that firsthand. Look at the healthy people in your life. They eat certain foods, sure, but they also have a certain attitude about themselves. True dedication to oneself takes place all the time, even when no one is watching. It rests in how you view yourself. For holistic health, you need to have a healthy attitude in addition to a healthy body.

Go stand naked in front of a mirror and tell yourself how beautiful you are without makeup or clothes. I'm serious. Go do it. Don't hide behind clothes or your bed or anything else between you and the reflective surface. Stand in front of the mirror plain, just you, naturally, in all your glory. It doesn't matter what size clothes you wear or whether you have the body you think you should have. You are exactly how God wanted you to be. I tell myself five things I love about myself every single day. It helps me. I promise you that if you love yourself, the words of others and the dark thoughts that sometimes swim into your consciousness will hold no power over you.

Love yourself unconditionally.

10

IDENTITY

Who am I, and why am I here?

This is one of the most complex questions that we will ever ask ourselves. Everyone agrees that we all have a purpose in life, but unless we take the time to know ourselves as individuals, we will never begin to understand the range of possibilities our lives' purposes can contain. There isn't anything I could say that would convince you that you inherently know what your purpose is here on earth—that's something you have to find yourself through introspection and exploration.

Who are you? Identity seems like a daunting topic, especially since others have already tried to identify you themselves. The instinct to identify the unknown is one of humanity's most basic characteristics— and everyone you meet is a puzzle to solve. Unfortunately, to make things easier, we often classify others in basic, shallow stereotypes. Suddenly, you're a loser, nerd, gay, fat, goth—the list goes on and on. You may feel limited to the stereotypes others have placed you in, but you need to remember that their opinions are irrelevant. You are not defined by people's first impressions of you.

Uncle Rick

One friend of my dad's, a dear role model of mine whom I call "Uncle Rick," is an inspiration to me for what it means to defy stereotypes and live above your label. Uncle Rick is paralyzed from the neck down. He was only a teenager when he lost the ability to walk and participate in daily activities. A high-school athlete with a promising future in sports, his dreams were seized from him in a sad twist of fate. But he's shown me that dreams can change. To this very day, my uncle hasn't let his disability slow him down. Through the Buoniconti Fund, which is also known as The Miami Project to Cure Paralysis, he has helped those who are also paralyzed. You can look up the project on their website, www.TheMiamiProject.org.

Uncle Rick turned his tragedy into something bigger than just him. He raises money by running golf tournaments and other events in order to give funds in excess of one million dollars back to people suffering from paralysis, just like him. At the Miami Project, they named a wing of the hospital after him: the Ricky Palermo and Palermo Family Foundation Spinal Cord Injury and Research Wing.

He inspires me to be a better person each and every day. I hope he knows how proud I am of him.

Uncle Rick didn't allow his label—that of a disabled man—to define him. He didn't succumb to the stereotype others immediately placed him in. He knows that he is a man who can help others, and he pursues this calling with all his heart. Uncle Rick, through difficulty and setbacks, knows who he is and what his purpose on earth is, and that makes him far better off than most people today.

You Are Not a Stereotype

Stereotypes have been around as long as people have existed. From the day you, as a baby, were able to look at something and try to figure out its purpose, you've been able to place people into stereotypes. It's a part of our genetics and contributes to the concept of "survival of the fittest." However, we'd be better off if people kept their comments to themselves. Taking an initial stab at identifying someone isn't necessarily bad, but when we voice those labels, we restrict others— and potentially the person we're speaking of—from embracing that person's full complexity and individuality. Beauty—like a lot of other qualities—is, after all, in the eye of the beholder.

Stereotypes can differ based upon many variables, such as race, sex, religion, and even morals. I've found that people of all ages are guilty of gender stereotypes. Young girls usually claim that boys are all jerks, and guys will state that girls are too emotional. Even when boys and girls become adults, the sex-based assumptions flow into the workforce. For example, it's common knowledge that men make more money than women. I don't understand why; we work the same amount, yet men are still seen as the superior gender.

I'm guilty of judging people based off appearance. I often look at people and ask myself, *What was going on in their head when they got dressed this morning?* Horrible, I know. Yet other people do it too. You can't stop people from trying to place you in a stereotype or give you a label, so instead, let's change how you view your own stereotype.

Discover Who You Are First; The Rest Will Follow

Who are you? You've been on a journey of self-exploration since your first day on this planet. You've grown from infant to child to young adult, and you're now at the crossroads of choices that will determine the direction you go in your future. You are faced with decisions such as where to go to school, what to study, and what career to pursue. It's a lot to take in. If you're overwhelmed, take it slow. You don't have to answer all of those things in one sitting. First examine who you are as an individual, and the rest will follow. There is no better goal in life than being able to understand who you are and what you have to offer. There are people who go their entire lives not knowing who they are or what they will do in this life.

Life will often put you in situations where the choice you make will reveal a bit about yourself. Don't avoid these situations; embrace them.

There's no way to know who you are until you are forced to learn. I let someone tell me who I was based on what I looked like and how they viewed me. For a long time, I believed them, too. I was afraid to be anyone other than who they told me I was. But ever since I started looking at myself and trying to pull my individual identity out of the images people cast on me, who I really am has become clearer. If you were to ask me today who I am in my entirety ... well, I still don't know the answer, but I'm closer to figuring it out.

Sometimes, I have no idea who I am. There are days on which I identify as a lone wolf and other days on which I want to be a part of something bigger than myself, like Uncle Rick. Sometimes I want to continue down the entertainment-industry path, but then there are days when I just want a normal lifestyle. Am I bipolar? I don't think so. I'm still riddling out who I am and what purpose I want to pursue in life. If you're like me and keep changing your mind, that doesn't mean there's something wrong with you. In fact, you should be proud. You're asking yourself the big questions now at a young age, and that puts you ahead of a lot of adults in life.

Understanding Your Influences

In an earlier chapter, we talked about what kind of people qualify as good friends. You want people who will lift you up, not tear you down. But another quality you want to find in a friend is someone who allows you to relax and just be *you*. There comes a time in your life when you start to intentionally choose your friends based on those who will help you succeed in life. That time is now. Not when you leave for college, not when summer break starts. Don't let school be the deciding factor in who gets to influence you.

Friends come and go. I know people say friendships last forever, but that's not the case. People change, and at the end of the day, all you have is yourself. You will be your own best friend and your biggest advocate until the day you die. The people with whom you surround yourself will either help you or hurt you. I've learned that you can put all you have into a friendship, but sometimes, even that isn't good enough. Sometimes people don't think of you the same way you think of them. You have to decide who is worthy of meeting the person you truly are.

Still having a hard time figuring out what kind of person you are beneath the labels? I'm going to try to help you find that person. Examine those you surround yourself with; it's never a bad idea to do a detox of negative people. Negativity will only bring you down and will prevent you from maximizing your experience on earth. Every choice you make has a consequence and a perk. Every relationship may contribute to your successes or may be your demise. The choices you make will allow you to find your happiness or to understand why you are not fully satisfied. However, if you stay true to yourself, then you should be able to learn what it is that allows you to blossom.

Think back to your childhood, when you knew without a doubt what you liked and what you didn't like. Aside from the fact that you are older, not much else has changed. Yes, you are more intelligent, you understand life a bit better, and you have experienced more, but the foundation of who you are will never change. For example, think of the things that inspired you as kid versus what inspires you now. I bet you can find some underlying similarities between the two.

As a kid, my first inspiration was—believe it or not—Tarzan. I wanted to soar through the sky, swing vine to vine, or proudly defeat my enemies. As I got older, my role models changed; no more superheroes, capes, or anything fake. I left childhood whimsy behind and instead looked up to the people in my life. I saw my future in my parents; I wanted to be like them. They seemed so happy and at ease with the life they had together. Little did I know how many battles they had fought. I'd only witnessed their happiness, their unconditional love for me, and the little lessons they tried to teach me.

I'm inspired by other things, too. I'm inspired by the wind, the way words speak to my soul, the way people interact, and how one action can change the world. I also love to read. I love anything that challenges my thoughts and makes me want to push myself further. Writers such as Charles Dickens, Stephenie Meyer, Suzanne Collins, Ron Howard, Barbara Hall, John Green, Nicholas Sparks, and Quentin Tarantino are a few of my favorites. All of them have something in common: they allow you to escape reality and fall into something magical. Despite their differences, and despite the different manners in which they convey their ideas, all authors have a message. When I write, I wish to tell a story—a story with which I can captivate an audience and deliver a meaningful, lasting message. My favorite authors have inspired me to write, and I owe them for igniting the creative spark in me. At the end of the day, I've learned what truly inspires me: helping others. I wish to have an impact on someone else's life, like others have had on mine.

Your inspirations are part of your identity. Find them, and you'll find yourself.

Happiness Is the Key

The key to finding yourself is to understand what makes you happy: the unique characteristics that make you who you are. If you are pretending to be someone you're not, are you really happy?

I tried to be someone I was not for the longest time. I pretended to like playing with dolls when I'd much rather have been outside. I stopped dressing up as Tarzan and became Princess Jasmine. As I got older, I hid my love for country music and listened to pop instead. I still pretend to be something I am not in front of certain people—it's part of my job—but those closest to me know the real me.

Here's the truth. Other than yourself, there is nothing stopping you from doing those things or being the person you really want to be. Stop acting, and let the real you come back. There's a possibility you have no idea who the person you want to be is or what makes you happy; you can lose sight of that. It's okay to lose sight every once in a while. Think about what you want to do for a profession when you are older. You probably have some answers ready, right? It's because it's a question we've been asked almost all our lives: "What do you want to be when you grow up?"

John Lennon once said, "When I went to school, they asked me what I wanted to be when I grew up. I wrote down 'happy.' They told me I didn't understand the assignment, and I told them they didn't understand life." We've been conditioned to find our identity in our careers and social status rather than our emotional composition. If a five-year-old John Lennon can think that way, what is stopping you?

Maybe the reason our generation struggles with its identity is because people have told us to be something we aren't or to define ourselves in terms of what we want to be—or want our path to be—at such a young age. I think people should be judged for how they view themselves or want to be seen. Being happy is a natural-born right. Yet within our own country and around the world alike, there is so much hate. People are so afraid of rejection that they go their entire lives settled into a mold they were shoved into at a young age. No one should ever just settle. But once again, fear stops us from living our lives to the fullest. So maybe instead of trying to figure out who you will be, figure out who you are. The rest will fall into place.

If we eliminate fear, we eliminate negativity. Once we do that, maybe we can accept who we are and embrace it. I stopped being scared of what people thought of me. If I want to dance in public, I will. If I want to skip through the halls of school, why shouldn't I? If I want to tell my best friend that I love him—well, I will. I've accepted who I am. I can accept who I am because I have no fear within myself of allowing my happiness to bloom.

So why shouldn't you be happy too? Do what makes you happy. If you can find something that makes you happy, people you love, and a job that you enjoy—what more could you want? You just have to be okay with the fact that finding these things may require you to put yourself in the uncomfortable position of demanding honesty. Not from others, but from yourself. For once, allow those feelings of discomfort when you're with your "friends" to speak to you. Recognize when you're looking in the mirror and see makeup that makes you look like a version of yourself you don't know. Acknowledge when you're stifling laughter or tears. Walk away from friendships that make you feel this way, and concentrate your time on finding people who celebrate your true identity.

It makes me sad to see people my own age or younger act like someone they're not. I've seen many young girls dressing provocatively to impress boys. Dress for yourself, not for others. If someone is going to like you, they will like you for you. Looks will only get you so far in life. The person you are on the inside—whether you try to hide that person or not—will come out eventually. If people choose not to like you because of the way you are, they should not be in your life.

146

Life is too short to find your identity in anything that isn't yourself. If you surround yourself with negative people, they will affect your outlook on life. Those people may even stop you from reaching your full potential in life, even if you are unsure of what that potential is.

The greatest gift that life has to offer is that no one gets to tell us who we are. You are you, and I am I. I can't say it enough: only you can control the direction your life will go in. In order to be successful and happy, you must try to block out the negativity that the world is so full of. Learn to embrace your callings, whatever they may be. Life is too short to not be happy or not pursue anything you want achieve.

Embrace your weirdness. Skip through halls, sing in the shower—whatever it is, do it. If you can look yourself in the mirror and tell yourself that you have nothing but love for who you are, then you're truly happy.

There Is Only One You in the World

Identity can seem like such a complex topic. However, when you take it and break it down, it ends up with you as an individual. Identity shapes how you view the world and affects your own outlook on life. It doesn't matter if you are seen as an outcast or as different; the world needs more of that. Do you think Steve Jobs, Mark Zuckerberg, or Bill Gates was sitting at the popular table at lunch? In such a dark place, we need people who can spark light in the once-great world.

Whatever stereotype the world has decided to give you, go out and prove it wrong. You can either allow your stereotype to define you, or you can show everyone why they were wrong. Words cannot define you. Only your actions define your true identity. The way you live and inspire those around you will show that words cannot dictate who you are. I've learned that the more I inspire others or share what I have to offer, the more complete I feel as a person. My soul is a complex place, just as yours is, and I've learned that I am truly happy when I can help others.

Seek happiness on your own. Find your passion. We all have different callings and are happiest when doing different tasks. Your own happiness will give you a reason to push on even in your darkest hours. If you can't seem to find happiness, take a look at your life as a whole.

Identity isn't so complex after all. I've learned that identity is just another word for happiness, and true happiness is self-acceptance. As Lucille Ball says, "Love yourself first, and everything else falls into line. You really have to love yourself to get anything done in this world." You're human; you're not supposed to be perfect. As long as you can look in a mirror and love the reflection looking back at you, you will be okay. Increasing your self-worth by truly celebrating who you are is the best form of affection anyone could ever give you. So be happy with yourself, find people who are happy with you, and don't let anyone try to change that. God made you as you were supposed to be made.

#BeenThere

I had always been a star athlete in middle school, so I was extra excited for the first day of softball tryouts my freshman year of high school. Unfortunately, during that schoolday, I sustained an injury that prevented me from trying out. I thought I would be completely bummed about this, but part of me was . . . relieved. I had always done everything to be part of the popular crowd. Being an athlete was cool in my school. However, I was not like the popular girls—those boy-crazy girls with baseball-player boyfriends and heels that came out of their bags when the cleats came off. I was more of a tomboy. I always had been, as a child, but I'd learned to hide it. I mean, I did not wear a skirt until sixth grade unless some begged me to. So what problem did I have with being on the team?

I now realize that I was afraid the "gay" would come out. I was already a member of the marching band's flag team, one of the girliest activities I could possibly have been part of, and was experiencing feelings for girls I had never had before—or at least never acknowledged. These feelings followed me throughout high school, even as I had boyfriends and skipped over activities and events that made me question my identity. Looking back now, I cannot believe I edited myself in that way.

I don't know that I would have come out earlier, but I certainly would not have stopped myself from enjoying the things I enjoyed or participating in the activities I knew I was good at for fear of what others might have thought. I was a great athlete, and I missed out on doing something I love because of fear. Fear of people not liking me and fear of someone seeing something in me I wasn't ready to see myself. Too many people in high school make choices based on other people's reactions, and that is no way to live. Stop caring what other people think! The decisions you make in high school help shape what you will become as an adult. These choices are not frivolous. If you love something, do it. Don't be afraid to join the chess team, the debate team, or the softball team. Always live proudly, and remember that the choices you make today will only make you a better and stronger person tomorrow. The homerun moment for this story: I now play in an all-girls LGBTQ softball league in New York City during the summers and get to relive the high-school glory days I foolishly opted out of. Live your life in the now, and opt out of *nothing!*

—Jennifer Perlmutter,

creative consultant, age thirty-one

11
COLLEGE AND OUR FUTURES BEYOND

Fear of the unknown is going to give me a heart attack one of these days. The future is one of the scariest things I've ever had to think about. No one knows what the future holds, and all of us, to a certain degree, are scared of it. Life would be so much simpler if we could live day to day, but instead we worry about what tomorrow will bring, and we worry whether our plans for the future will be enough to help us fulfill our purposes in life.

As I think about the distant future, my mind automatically jumps to death. It's morbid, but true. We're all going to die someday, and as time progresses, we arrive closer to the day that will be our last. I used to wake up in the morning wondering if I'd live to see tomorrow. It's hard not to think about the possibility that I could die in a car accident, have a massive heart attack, choke, etc.—the mortal list is almost infinite. There's no point in worrying about the things we can't control. But I've seen so many deaths and close calls just in the past year alone that I'm a little fearful.

A few months ago, my parents went on a cruise out of the country for the weekend. They gave me emergency contact numbers "just in case." On their way out of the door, I reassured them, "Everything will be okay! Nothing bad will happen." But as Murphy's law would have it, that *would* be the weekend something traumatic occurred. The weekend started off normal: no sense of forthcoming doom looming over the house, just a list of chores and a box of cereal. Like most things in life, everything went perfectly smoothly until I was thrown a curveball.

The day after Halloween, I woke up early to get a head start on the chores I was supposed to do in my parents' absence. I had to move boxes that belonged to my grandmother, who lived in an assisted living facility, from the garage into the attic. I ran up and down the stairs carrying boxes for a solid hour. My Sunday seemed to be off to a productive start . . . and then the phone rang.

Gram's assisted living location popped up on the screen. Nothing abnormal. She called multiple times on a daily basis, so I didn't rush to the phone. Instead, I waltzed over to pick it up, expecting to hear her voice. However, I was not greeted by my grandmother's familiar tone. The strange voice asked if my parents were home, and I explained that they were out of the country. The woman on the other end seemed pretty concerned, so I asked if anything had happened. She told me she couldn't tell me because I wasn't eighteen yet. My heart began to race.

As I begged for more information, adrenaline rushed through my body. I could hear the panic in my voice as I pleaded for her to make an exception, just one time. She was hesitant at first, but then she asked me to remain on the line for a few moments. After what felt like hours, she returned to the phone. The woman cleared her throat, and I heard a new tone in her voice as she told me that my grandmother had been taken by ambulance to a hospital earlier that morning. She told me that that was all the information she could legally offer and that I would have to find out the rest on my own.

I ran across the street for help from my neighbors, but—just my luck—they weren't home. I then dashed back into my house and called my boyfriend's mother, who lived a few doors down. After I explained what had happened, we made phone calls together to the surrounding hospitals. After a short while, we found out that Gram was in the emergency room at Orlando Regional Medical Center. I jumped in the shower for less than a minute, threw on clothes, and jumped in my car—still soaking wet.

I have never driven so fast in my entire life. At the time, I didn't care if a police officer pulled me over. I was the only family member in the state who could help my grandma. My boyfriend's mother came with me because she worried that I'd need assistance getting access to my grandma. We lied to the attendant, telling the man that my boyfriend's mother was my aunt, so that she could gain entry to the emergency room. After they scanned our licenses and took our photo, we were escorted into the ward. As we were walking to my grandmother's room, we saw a body roll by on a gurney. The man's face was covered, and he was escorted by a police officer. When they passed, I immediately felt ill. Then I saw my grandmother, asleep in the next room over.

She looked peaceful, despite the fact that she was hooked up to an IV and heart monitor. As I saw her weak body lying there, my heart heaved in sympathy. I knew she was in good hands, but she must have been in so much pain. My greatest fear was that she had felt very alone throughout this experience. I woke her gently and held her hand. She told me that she had fallen getting out of bed and had remained on the floor for three hours before someone in the assisted living facility found her. I can't fathom how scared she must have been that no one would find her at all.

After a few hours, a doctor came into the room and delivered the news I had feared. She told us that Gram had broken her femoral neck (where the ball and socket meet in the hip) and would need a partial hip replacement as soon as possible. The doctor then asked me to sign on my grandmother's behalf to proceed with surgery. She pulled me to the side and told me about the risks of the surgery—how it would be difficult due to Gram's age and frail body. I had two choices: I could sign the papers to allow them to go through with the hip replacement so that Gram would be able to walk again. This option was almost sure to improve her quality of life if she stuck with the program after surgery. Or I could choose not to sign the papers and instead wait till my parents got home. However, this could mean Gram would lose the ability to walk.

Deciding whether to wait until my parents returned or give the go ahead to put my Gram through surgery was by far the hardest decision I've ever had to make. The most difficult part of it all was figuring out how I would relay the news to my parents. I wished my parents could have been there to help me through the process, but they weren't. However, a day later, they returned. The final papers were then signed, and my grandmother went into surgery.

Murphy's Law is a bitch. Fate doesn't wait to encroach upon a life; death and accidents are all around us. I am thankful my grandmother is okay, because if anything had gone wrong, I don't know how I would've broken the news to my parents upon their return. My three days spent in the hospital made me realize how weak the human body is. We don't live forever, but I don't have any fear of dying. I know we all return to whatever it is we came from. If God chooses to take me today or a month from now, I'll know that I've lived a great life. I can only pray that I will live a life of longevity and happiness.

Looking at the Immediate Future

However, the future isn't just about death. For many of us, death is the last thing on our minds as we worry about something that affects our more immediate future: college.

Like a lot of you, I'm currently in a hell-bound limbo otherwise known as senior year. Senior year always seemed so far away, but now it's finally come around. It's a year in which we must choose whether to go to college, which society has deemed the safer path, or to take a deep breath and decide to design a path for ourselves.

I'd always looked forward to my last year of high school. I was never a fan of school, but I was under the impression that senior year was going to be the best time of my life. After all, it is, technically speaking, the last required year of formal education.

As a kid, I assumed that all the seniors would be friends, bound together by all we had accomplished together during our time in school. That's funny to me now because I never got to experience that camaraderie—or even a typical last year in class. I didn't have a "normal" senior year, full of bonding and a relaxed schedule. While most seniors were wrapping up their high-school credits, socializing, and going to pep rallies, I wasn't. Instead, I was writing a book, learning a full film script, traveling, trying to pass my college entry exams, and taking online college courses on top of all that.

I'm not trying to complain—I'm happy this way. I like being busy. The choices I've made in my short eighteen years define me. They contribute to my unique identity. I chose to write because I felt it was the only way to open up about my own experiences. And I've discovered that writing a book is no easy task. Three years ago, if someone were to ask me whether I'd consider writing something this big, I would've laughed. It's kind of like my relationship with acting. I hated acting and public speaking in middle school, but now I'm currently shooting a movie. When I jumped into professional acting and worked with some of the best coaches in the business, I began to realize that acting wasn't as terrifying as I'd thought. It was actually a way to be someone I wasn't for a short amount of time; it became an escape. It's ironic that we can be so opposed to something one day and then end up loving it the next. We should always be open to trying new opportunities. You never know how they may affect your future.

The Evolution of Education

Education can be an intimidating topic. It is, after all, the foundation of our entire lives when we're young. We were thrown onto the fresh pavement of the learning system from preschool age, ready to ride. Preschool was a lighthearted experience meant to set the ball rolling for our future. It was a time in which we played with blocks and learned our ABCs — all of which had a monumental impact on our minds today. At the time, we never realized how quickly we'd be using this knowledge—how quickly all the seemingly meaningless information in our young minds would be called upon on a daily basis. We had no idea what life had in store for us or what potential our brain capacity could reach. Day by day, as we got older, we found ourselves at the mercy of knowledge—and we're still at that mercy.

The warmth of love we received from our teachers in preschool was short lived, because soon we transitioned to kindergarten. In kindergarten, we were able to have leisurely naps, play at recess, and learn catchy songs. It was also the time in which we, as "little people," learned the fundamentals of social encounters. Kindergarten allowed us to freely make friends we could cherish for a lifetime.

Elementary school followed a short year after, and the foundation we'd built in kindergarten became the cornerstone for the rest of our education. The years that made up elementary school were merely a learning experience, teaching us to establish responsibility and a routine of waking up in the morning, arriving to school on time, doing homework, and following directions.

When middle school finally came around, the routines got more difficult. We were required to complete tests, take home lengthy work, play sports, and stay out of social drama. Middle school made up some of my most difficult years. I didn't really fit in with the other students, I was kind of socially awkward, and it was hard for me to pay attention in class. I always did the work the teachers assigned, but when it came time to apply myself socially, I struggled.

School itself wasn't the problem; the problem was the atmosphere at school. The drama conflicted with learning and altered my perception of what school should be like. I was so focused on fitting in that I let my grades slip—and for what? To sit at the popular kids' table?

Let me just tell you: those who sat at that table will never fully leave their school lives behind. They'll forever feed off feeling superior to others, yet they'll be unequipped when the umbilical cord of popularity is cut. Until I finally got to that table, I didn't realize how fake and insecure they truly were, always having to compliment each other or hang out all the time. They weren't comfortable being by themselves. They'd even gossip about one another in each other's absence. I finally realized how obsolete it all was. I got to sit at the popular table for a short time, and I wonder what they said about me when I got up and never returned.

When middle school finally ended, I was ecstatic. I loved the thought of going to high school. I was ready to pick classes that interested me and surround myself with people I could hold conversations with. For the first month of my freshman year, I was awarded this privilege. However, it ended after the second month, when I was approached in the mall by the modeling scout. I never got to be part of the normal high-school experience that everyone later talks about with nostalgia in their hearts.

My life took an alternate route. Most of the time, I found myself in an online classroom so I could complete assignments while traveling. When I was home, I attended school in person. I was enrolled in the same private school from kindergarten all the way through my senior year of high school. If you were to pull up my attendance record, however, you'd see that it was a rarity that I ever physically made it to class. On the rare days I could actually sit in a classroom, I loved every minute of it. To me, there's something in the act of learning that is unlike any other feeling—whether it comes from absorbing knowledge from an educational higher power or helping someone else discover the joy of learning something new.

Although I didn't spend as much time in a classroom as you likely did, I certainly experienced the same pressures we all face in senior year. The guidance counselors breathe down your neck about the college application process. The hands you held on to since preschool finally let go, and now you're on own. It's horrifying to ask yourself, "Am I good enough?" I feel that is the question we all ask when we apply to schools . . . a question that is answered in the blunt form of a rejection or an acceptance letter.

Getting into College

The funny thing about high school is that everyone has the same plan: go to a great college, get a great job, make a lot of money, and settle down. After doing my college applications, I realized that I was competing against students from all over the world. These students all wanted the same thing I did: to get into the school of their choice. As you know, however, getting into college is not quite that easy. Completing college applications gave me my first real look at how difficult life was going to be after school. It doesn't matter what you've accomplished or how great of a person you are; if you don't fit certain criteria, your chances drop. When the smart kids started to panic, I had an "oh shit" moment.

The moment I realized the rest of my life was going to be every man for himself, I drafted alternate plans. If I couldn't get into the college of my choice, I could always go get my associate in arts (AA) from a community college and then transfer. I could travel while I completed two years of school before settling into a four-year institution. For another backup plan, I even considered not going to college, like my father. However, that doesn't seem like the right option for me.

I would love to tell you that you will get into the school of your dreams, but unfortunately, I can't say that. Rejection is a part of life, and handling rejection with grace is a skill we all have to learn at some point. Even if you don't get into an Ivy League school, you can still get a respectable education. We all have our strengths and weakness—not everyone is an Einstein. Colleges understand that we're all different, and they don't look just at our grades. They also look at our achievements and see our interests and hobbies. If a school doesn't select you, don't take it personally. They're looking for people who fit their particular atmosphere, and if they don't think you'd be a good fit, then it's probably better for you in the long run.

The college application process can seem daunting, especially when you have to take entry exams like the ACT or SAT. If you're like me, you may not be able to focus when you're in a room full of people. My automatic response to sitting in a crowded environment like that is to focus absolutely anywhere in the room other than the test in front of me. When I finally look down at the bubble maze before me, I draw a blank on all the material I've ever learned. When panicked like this, I want to feed off people's energy for encouragement, but when you're sitting next to ill people, you get sick too.

I know that no one is fond of college entry exams. They are the scariest tests I have ever had to take. I highly suggest getting a tutor or at least buying the practice tests. I bought a book: *The Real ACT*. It had sample tests and strategies for me to study. I never picked up a copy of an SAT-geared aid, but I've been told by my school counselors that the *Official SAT Study Guide* is the best tool for review.

The first college exam I took was the SAT. Someone told me I might do better on it than on the ACT, so I didn't study or look at any sample materials. Worst decision of my entire life. I thought the test would cover common knowledge, but no.

As I left the testing room a mere four hours later, I decided that that was not the test for me and that I would try the ACT. I had heard it was easier—also false. My parents invested in a tutor and all the practice books we could find, yet I still managed to do poorly on my exams. I got a solid 1480 out of 2400 on the SAT, and a 24 out of 36 on the ACT. As I stated before, I can't take a test to save my life.

Since taking the ACT and SAT are very real things we all have to do, I'd advise that you get a tutor, as tutors help immensely. I learned to think of the test as a chess game, all about strategy. The answers are all in front of you, and tutors hone in on how to select the right answer through process of elimination. When you show up to take the test, try not to talk to people. They're horrified, and their negative energy will lead to a panic attack. At this point in your life, you cannot afford a panic attack. Don't underestimate the ACT or SAT; I did, and I honestly shouldn't have. I'd like to sit here and comment on how absurd it is to use standardized testing for college admissions, but I'll leave that for you to reflect upon instead.

After your test scores, the next thing colleges will see about you is your GPA. It's the culmination of all your hard work as a student. When it comes to GPA, my advice is to try your best. The grades you get in high school are a large factor in which colleges will accept you as an incoming student. IB, AP, and honors classes will boost your GPA higher than a standard class that uses a 4.0 scale. Many different schools offer these programs to provide a more rigorous course load. I have been told by my college advisors that it looks better to choose a schedule that will push your academics to new heights. However, keep in mind that you should be able to do well in the classes you pick. It will not benefit you in any way if you choose the hardest class and pull through with a C. Take classes that you know will challenge you but that allow you to maintain an A or B average.

I can't tell you that you will automatically get good grades if you study hard, because that's definitely not the case. Some people are just more academically inclined than others. I studied hard, but I'm still no Einstein. My strong suits were volunteering, clubs, and extracurricular activities. I even confessed in my application that I struggled with certain subjects but that I always tried my best. If you challenge yourself, college admissions officers will see that as a strength, not as a defect.

No matter what your test scores or GPA look like, you still have a shot at your preferred college when you fill out the application itself. The college essay is practically an interview on paper, and it's the only portion of the application in which you get to explain what makes you the best candidate for the school. Don't let yourself be defined solely by your academic talents. The college admissions officer is a person too, and he or she wants to be able to connect with you. Let your words tell your story, and convince the admissions officer why the school needs someone like you on its campus.

The essay is my favorite part of the college application process because I have always loved to write. I know many of you reading this dread writing essays. That doesn't surprise me. However, this essay is your only chance to connect with an admissions officer before all your hard work goes into a stack on his or her desk. Don't allow yourself to become just another piece of paper in a pile of many. You have a story. Tell it. Talk about what makes you who you are. Let the officers see who you are and why they need you at their schools.

Embrace Your Opportunities

College is going to be an experience in itself. It's not only the first time in our lives we are on our own but also the first time we get to decide what we do with our time and energy. No one else can make those decisions for us. Regardless of where you go to get an education, you'll receive an experience unlike any other you've had before. I've been told that the friends you make in college will be there for you for the rest of your life. I have not yet gone to college, obviously, but I know it will be the best time of my life. The college I attend will become a home away from home, and the people I will meet will shape me as an emerging adult.

The thought of leaving your parents behind at home to go away to school may be difficult, but part of life is growing up and moving on. I know you may be scared. I am too. At one point, your parents were moving out of your grandparents' homes for the first time, and they were scared as well. However, your family isn't going anywhere. They will still be there when you're on school breaks, when you have a rough week and need to go home for the weekend, and when you graduate. College is one of the largest stepping-stones you will cross in your lifetime, and your parents are encouraging you to go because they want what's best for you.

When my parents and I talk about me going away to school, sometimes they act as though we have forever to talk about it, and sometimes I feel this urgency that makes it seem like college is right around the corner. I don't know what it's like to let go of your child in this crazy world; I can only imagine. Truthfully, I think I'm more scared than they are. I hope they realize that they have raised me to be exactly who they wanted me to be. I want them to be proud of their accomplishments instead of sad to say good-bye, because, without them, I wouldn't have made it this far.

Every so often, I sit my parents down on the couch and reassure them that they have done their job and should be commended for that. No matter how far away I am from them, I will still be their baby girl. Our parents will always be a huge part of what defines our home, no matter how old we get. I believe I can speak for many of us when I say that although the love we have for our parents is immense, we often don't show it. It will be hard for them to let us go away to college; it probably feels as though it was only yesterday that they were dropping us off at preschool for the first time. Yet here we are. It's time to let go.

College is a big step in this crazy thing called life. There are days I wish I could be on my own, but then there are days I wish I didn't have to leave my parents. But I know I will eventually have to. I know I need to move on and start a life of my own. I want to meet people and experience the world, but I never want to let go of those I love now. Your childhood home will always be your home, but you need to go out and experience all this world has to offer.

Go to college. Pursue your dreams. Maybe even do a semester abroad. I want to do that. I want to study in some foreign place. Experiencing another culture is a form of education unto itself. People all operate differently, and there are many things we can learn from each other. There are so many different things we end up doing with our lives because we are not alike. We are not supposed to be alike. There's no cookie cutter that formed us. There is no perfect person. We all have flaws. We all have our own perfections. We simply fit the mold that God created for each of us individually.

Life Beyond College

Your friends may not get into the same college as you, but that does not mean you can't still be friends. I know some people follow friends or significant others to college just to be with them, but true friends will remain with you no matter where you go. Don't go to a school you do not want to attend just to be with your friends—never let that be the sole factor when it comes to deciding where you want to receive your education. Go to the school that *you* want to go to—one that will be beneficial to your career. You will meet new people and create new relationships regardless of where you go in life. College is a time to meet people and try something new. It's all what you make of it.

So when you begin to submit your college applications, have faith in yourself. You'll end up at the college you're meant to attend. But that doesn't mean you shouldn't have a backup plan in case you don't get into the school of your dreams. You could always transfer later on. Do not give up on your education. It doesn't matter what level of education you have or have not yet achieved; it's never too late to go back to school if you want to. School is not meant to determine what you can and cannot do with your life. Your level of education should not define you. If you do not attend college, chase your dreams. You can do anything you set your mind to, but I guarantee a diploma does help, especially because your dreams and goals may change as you continue to grow as a person with every year you're on this earth.

Despite all my primary and backup plans, I don't know what the future holds for me. The plans I so carefully drew up may come crashing down on me, but I want to believe that I'm ready for any situation life will throw at me. I haven't the slightest idea what I want to do with the rest of my life. When I ask my friends and peers what their plans are, they seem to know what they want to do and how they're going to do it.

I've changed my mind more than ten times about my potential career choice. When I was around ten, I wanted to be a history teacher. At age thirteen, I wanted to be an FBI agent. At fourteen, I wanted to be a model and then an actress. In fact, after spending some time modeling, I did fly out to Los Angeles and sign with Mavrick Artists Agency in order to pursue a career in the entertainment industry. Soon after, at the age of seventeen, I booked a lead role in a horror movie called *Sweethearts*, which is currently in development. Throughout all of this, however, I was still in high school and still considering different options for my future career. Now, at eighteen, I've decided that I'd ideally like to be a writer of some sort. However, I'm quite sure the list will continue.

In my experience, some of the wealthiest people are also the unhappiest. When I commit full time to the workforce, I want to do something that I know will benefit me, regardless of how much money I make. I don't want to spend the rest of my life being miserable. My mom has always said, "I'll love you even if you decide you want to pick up dog poop for the rest of your life—as long as it makes you happy." Well, luckily for my mother, I don't plan to do that. I'm sure that, with time, I will settle into a concrete plan of what I want to do professionally. I'm not scared about the career I will take on. Everything will fall into place as it's meant to.

When I think about my own future, I don't care if I have the highest-paying job, the nicest car, or the most luxurious home. I just want to be happy. Until recently, I've not been as close with my family as I am now, so from this moment on, I want to make it a priority to have my family close to me. Someday, I want to start a family of my own with a loving husband. I hope this happens, but then again, you never know.

The flukes that we experience in life alter who we are as people. The past few years have shaped me into who I am today. My values have changed, and I've discovered that the point in living is to make the best out of the moments we experience. In the past, when I woke up in the morning, I would wonder if it were my last day on this earth. But I don't think this way anymore. When I wake up now, I wonder what I can do that day to make sure I've given myself every opportunity possible. Life is too short not to live in the moment. I've stopped worrying about the things I can't control; I know it's out of my hands and that everything happens for a reason. So make the most out of every single day you are given, because, as Nickelback once sang, "Each day's a gift and not a given right."

EPILOGUE

When I first thought of the concept for *Blatantly Honest*, I had only one goal in mind: to help. You now know some of my deepest, darkest secrets. I have no shame in telling you them. For the privacy of the others involved, I have chosen to leave out names. It is my way of taking the high road. But I can live with every choice I have made, and I wouldn't change anything that has happened to me.

In writing this book, I did not sit behind a computer screen seeking attention for my so-called "abnormal" life. I did not write this for sympathy, money, or anything else of that nature. I am driven solely by my will to help others. While writing, I realized that, by revisiting some of the most difficult times I've had to face, maybe I could help someone else. I hope that someone is you.

As I sit here wracking my brain for closing thoughts, I wonder whether I have done you any justice. I can only hope that my words have resonated deep within you in ways similar words never have before. There is always the chance that my words came across as something your mom or annoying older sister would say. But perhaps, for some odd reason, you listened to me. Perhaps you have now realized that your mom or sister was right but that you chose to ignore them. Maybe the reason you listened to me was obvious: I related to you.

I am just a teenager. Everyone is, at one point in his or her life. I was still in my teens, however, when I discovered I had a message that needed be shared with the world. I want to believe that this message came from something far greater than myself. Perhaps this "something" compelled me to write. Maybe I am a scribe in the eyes of God, or maybe I am just a girl who has an opinion louder than most. Regardless of the source of my message, I took a shot in the dark—for you.

Currently, there are almost eight billion people on the earth, but only a select few have attempted to explain what it means to live through the teenage stage of life. Why? Perhaps because it is nearly impossible to thoroughly discuss every issue a teenager may encounter. Sitting down to an empty screen and trying to somehow isolate the most important topics that teens face was a daunting task—a task that would have been much easier to just walk away from in fear of failure.

In complete honesty, I feel I have failed to define the whole teenage condition. Some of my own expertise will not account for what many people have experienced or will experience. Nor could I disclose other important topics that should have been addressed. (Maybe I will get a chance to in my next book.) It would be nearly impossible to please everyone, given that we all have different opinions on what is worth mentioning. But here's the difference: I tried.

My message to take away from this book is simple: the choices we make as teenagers affect who we'll become when we are older. My goal here is not to scare you about life in general or the flukes that can happen to you, because that list is almost infinite. Flukes do happen—that is a given—but how we react to them defines who we are. Our true identities have been written in the stars all along, and the choices we make lead us on our own personal journeys of discovery.

My life thus far has been anything but normal. I have had to make life-altering decisions and take risks. I may be different, but I can be just as easy to relate to as any other teen. Just like you, I have had many ups and downs, especially during the past five years. I too have had days when I wanted to throw in the towel, as well as days when I felt like I was on top of the world. I am sure you can relate. In the end, I have concluded that I am not a coward, I am not weak, and I don't wish my life had been different.

I have learned that many teenagers take their lives for granted. I know I almost did. We think we are invincible and that we're mature enough to make our own decisions. We're so anxious to become adults, be on our own, and break free from our parents' rules that we forget we only experience this stage once in a lifetime. We are so caught up in who we want to be that we forget who we are. This absentmindedness can lead to mistakes such as drugs, addictions, bullying, and one-night stands. Learn from them.

No one is perfect. There will be times when life throws you that dreaded curveball, and you'll have to choose whether to take it head on or run away. Sometimes the choice will not be clear. Making the wrong choice the first time does not make you a bad person. We all make the wrong choice from time to time.

In the end, we will all face what can feel like hell. When you realize that you're in such a place, you will wonder how you messed up—but only you will know what you did. Take responsibility for your actions. I wish I could tell you that life will get better right away. What I can tell you—and what I have been trying to tell you—is that, someday, you will know exactly who you are. Hopefully, you will have learned from your mistakes and will be able to distinguish the difference between right and wrong. I can only hope that you have learned something valuable from me—from the words of a fellow teenager.

NOTES

1. National Education Association, "Nation's Educators Continue Push for Safe, Bully-Free Environments," news release, October 8, 2012, http://www.nea.org/home/53298.htm.

2. "Statistics @ NVEEE," National Voices for Equality, Education and Enlightenment, accessed July 21, 2016, http://www.nveee.org/statistics/.

3. Ibid.

4. "Popping Pills: Prescription Drug Abuse in America," National Institute on Drug Abuse, National Institutes of Health, US Department of Health and Human Services, last modified January 2014, https://www.drugabuse.gov/related-topics/trends-statistics/infographics/popping-pills-prescription-drug-abuse-in-america.

ABOUT THE AUTHOR

Makaila Nichols started her modeling career at age fourteen, when she signed with respected agency Wilhelmina Models International. Since then, she's juggled school, modeling, a budding acting career, and now her newfound passion for writing. She accomplishes all this while traveling between New York and Los Angeles for work and then home to Florida for school and family. She is now a student at the University of Central Florida and a member of the Beta Lambda chapter of Delta Delta Delta. Her entertainment career continues to thrive, and she's now represented by a renowned theatrical agency and a high-fashion modeling agency in the Big Apple.

Although Makaila's life has been anything but ordinary, she faces many of the same challenges as other teens. In her debut book,

Blatantly Honest, she hopes to reach other young people by sharing her insights and advice on handling common teenage problems such as friends, dating, sex, and bullying. To contact Makaila, please visit www.MakailaNichols.com.

Makaila is also proud to serve as National Ambassador for The Great American NO BULL Challenge.

The Great American NO BULL Challenge is a 501 (c) (3) leadership and social activation organization using the power of filmmaking combined with social media to inspire positive change.

Get involved and be the change at www.NoBull.org.

PHOTOS

I couldn't resist. I feel like everyone needs a baby photo,
and this happens to be one of my favorites.

I played middle on the JV Volleyball team at school in eighth grade.

My callback cards after walking in the Fox Models International showcase.

Ice cream is a favorite food of mine in general, and this photo shows
that I love it—despite what many people would think.

Intense cycling workout before going to Miami for a weigh-in. In order to lose a few more pounds, I wore a sweat suit, sweatshirt, and sweatpants. The bucket next to me was used for spitting saliva into to shed a few more pounds of water weight.

Family photo.

Wilhelmina Models International contract signing
at the Mondrian Hotel in Miami, Florida.

First test shoot, shot by Lucie Hugary in Miami, Florida (fourteen years old).

The last photo I have with my wonderful Papa Fred. Rest in peace, Papa.

My first New York Fashion Week show at Pier 59 for fashion designer
John Paul Ataker's 2016–2017 Fall/Winter Collection.

Another favorite from a recent photo shoot.

High-fashion photo shoot with photographer Kristia Knowles.

Beauty shoot with Luis Quezada.

Father–daughter moment before red carpet in Los Angeles, California.

Never a bad time to spend quality time with Mom,
even if it is during a snowstorm in Central Park, New York City.

A typical fashion photo shoot with Kristia.

One of my favorite acting headshots, because I see
myself in this photo: a carefree girl with a dream.

My overwhelming first interaction with the press. What an experience . . .

Recent contract with One Management,
based in New York City, in the subdivision One.1.

ファッションの域を超えて。

ファッションデザインだけでなく総
合的なクリエイティブ集団として知
られ、波に乗っているアクネ。ス
トライプの構築的なイヴニングド
レスは、柄を微妙にずらしてオブ

High-fashion photo shoot with photographer Gail Hadani.

I had to get a press shot on the red carpet before
walking in Macy's Presents Fashion's Front Row, televised on E!

Windermere Preparatory's Prom King and Queen in 2016.